BIBLE STUDY COMMENTARY

Genesis and Exodus

Bible Study Commentary

Genesis and Exodus

A.E. CUNDALL

ARK PUBLISHING
130 City Road, London EC1V 2NJ

CHRISTIAN LITERATURE CRUSADE
Fort Washington, Pennsylvania 19034

©1981 Ark Publishing (UK dist.)
130 City Road, London EC1V 2NJ

Christian Literature Crusade (USA dist.)
Box C, Ft. Washington, PA 19034

First published 1981

ISBN 0 86201 083 7 (UK)
ISBN 0 87508 150 9 (USA)

Maps: Jenny Grayston

Phototypeset in Great Britain by
Filmtype Services Limited, Scarborough
Printed in U.S.A.

General Introduction

The worldwide church in the last quarter of the twentieth century faces a number of challenges. In some places the church is growing rapidly and the pressing need is for an adequately trained leadership. Some Christians face persecution and need support and encouragement while others struggle with the inroads of apathy and secularism. Christians must come to terms with the challenges presented by Marxism, Humanism, a belief that 'science' can conquer all the ills of mankind, and a whole range of Eastern religious and modern sects. If we are to make anything of this confused and confusing world it demands a faith which is solidly biblical.

Individual Christians, too, in their personal lives face a whole range of different needs – emotional, physical, psychological, mental. As we think more and more about our relationships with one another in the body of Christ and as we explore our various ministries in that body, as we discover new dimensions in worship and as we work at what it means to embody Christ in a fallen world we need a solid base. And that base can only come through a relationship with Jesus Christ which is firmly founded on biblical truth.

The Bible, however, is not a magical book. It is not enough to say, 'I believe' and quote a few texts selected at random. We must be prepared to work with the text until our whole outlook is moulded by it. We must be ready to question our existing position and ask the true meaning of the word for us in our situation. All this demands careful study not only of the text but also of its background and of our culture. Above all it demands prayerful and expectant looking to the Spirit of God to bring the word home creatively to our own hearts and lives.

This new series of books has been commissioned in response to the repeated requests for something new to follow on from Bible Characters and Doctrines. It is now over ten years since the first series of Bible Study Books were produced and it is hoped they will reflect the changes of the last ten years and bring the Bible text to life for a new generation of readers. The series has three aims:

1. To encourage regular, systematic personal bible reading. Each volume is divided into sections ideally suited to daily use, and will normally provide material for three months (the exceptions being Psalms and 1 Corinthians-Galatians, four months, and Mark and Ezra-Job, two months). Used in this way the books will cover the entire Bible in five years. The comments aim to give background information and enlarge on the meaning of the text, with special reference to the contemporary relevance. Detailed questions of application are however often left to the reader. The questions for further study are designed to aid in this respect.

2. To provide a resource manual for group study. These books do not provide a detailed plan for week by week study. Nor do they present a group leader with a complete set of ready-made questions or activity ideas. They do, however, provide the basic biblical material and, in the questions for further discussion they give starting points for group discussion.

3. To build into a complete Bible commentary. There is, of course, no shortage of commentaries. Here, however, we have a difference. Rather than look at the text verse by verse the writers examine larger blocks of text, preserving the natural flow of the original thought and observing natural breaks.

Writers have based their comments on the RSV and some have also used the New International Version in some detail. The books can, however, be used with any version.

GENESIS
Introduction

The Hebrew title, 'In the beginning', comes from the first word of the book. Our English title, 'Genesis', derives from the Septuagint meaning 'origin', or 'beginning'. Both titles are highly appropriate, for Genesis witnesses to the origin of this world; of man in relationship to God and to his fellows; of sin and judgement; of faith and sacrifice.

Genesis divides into two uneven sections. From ch.11 onwards it is biographical, dealing fully with the patriarchs Abraham, Isaac, Jacob and Joseph. God's call to Abraham was obviously the decisive point, where the great divine plan of redemption commenced, as witnessed by such 'credal' statements as, 'A wandering Aramean was my father . . .' (Deut. 26:5; compare Josh. 24:2-13). In contrast, throughout the rest of the Old Testament, there is remarkably slight reference to Gen. 1-11, where so much of vital 'pre-history' is compressed. Are these chapters unimportant therefore? By no means, for, in a remarkable way, they contain *all* that we need to know for an understanding of the redemptive drama which began to unfold with Abraham's call. To describe these chapters as a 'prologue' may be found helpful, especially as the essence of a prologue is to set out briefly an *accurate background*, which assumes a reliability and *essential historicity*.

Many scholars today, abandoning or modifying radically the literary division of the Graf-Wellhausen (or JEDP) hypothesis, approach the structure of Genesis via the phrase, 'These are the generations of . . .'. This phrase, occurring ten times (5:1;6:9;10:1;11:10,27;25:12,19; 36:1,9;37:2), divides the book into eleven sections. S. R. Driver (*The Book of Genesis*, Westminster Commentary) observed that this formed a framework for the entire narrative, and held that it became increasingly selective, with the aim of concentrating attention upon 'the immediate line of Israel's ancestors'. There is a probability that the phrase marks the owner or writer of the tablet ending (or less likely, beginning) with these words, and may witness to the original clay tablets, some of which accompanied the patriarchs on their journeyings, which were used in the compilation of Genesis.

For further details on the various critical issues raised you are referred to: (*a*) *Genesis*, (Tyndale Old Testament Commentary) by Derek F. Kidner; (*b*) the relevant sections in R. K. Harrison's, *Introduction to the Old Testament* (which has a value beyond a study of Genesis and Exodus). Representative critical viewpoints are reflected in E. A. Speiser, *Genesis* (Anchor Bible) or G. von Rad, *Genesis* (SCM Old Testament Library).

Analysis of Genesis

1:1-25 In the beginning

There is a unique majesty about the Genesis account of creation. Much has been made about its alleged connections with the Babylonian account, *Enuma elish*, but in fact, apart from a similar, common-sense order of creation, there are few connections. Another ancient epic, *Atraharsis*, is marginally closer to Genesis because it covers both Creation and Flood, but again there are fundamental differences. The heathen mythology is affected by its inadequate view of God. This in turn influences the understanding of every other relationship between the deity and the world in general, *and* with man.

In stark contrast, Genesis introduces us to an already-existing, uncreated God. No attempt is made to explain him. There is no conflict between God and the forces of chaos, as in the heathen accounts; nor is God in any way identified or confused with the whole, or any part, of creation, as were the ancient nature gods. He is absolutely sovereign in nature. It follows that what we term 'natural law', the rhythm and order set in the universe, is the expression of his will. Col. 1:16,17 underlines these truths, *and* affirms God's continuing rule. Note too the much-repeated statement, 'And God saw that it was good' (12,18,21,25). Man's sin disrupted society, and even affected the natural world (Gen. 3:17-19), but God's creation remains good, and to be *enjoyed* (1 Tim. 4:4).

Attempts have been made to reconcile the statements of Gen. 1 with our considerable but still increasing – and therefore tentative – scientific knowledge. This is understandable, since man is a questioning being. But there are dangers. Science and religion ought, properly, to be in partnership rather than in conflict. Science should open up our understanding of the natural world, but there is a realm which transcends this, in which science has no competence to make dogmatic pronouncements. Equally foolish is the theologian who closes his mind to the scientists' insights. Gen. 1 puts the focus upon God and his creation, but tells us little of the *mechanics* of creation. Such selectivity indicates where we should concentrate our *attention*, but the 'elasticity' of the account leaves ample room for the proven facts, if not the speculations, of scientific investigation. Ultimately, as Heb. 11:3 makes clear, our acceptance that 'the worlds have been framed by the word of God' is 'by faith', but what a well-founded faith!

TO THINK OVER: Faith, believing that God, the great Creator, is in perfect control of so vast and intricate a world, accepts that he is well able to take care of his children, and that the one who was already there, 'In the beginning' (1) can control our every new beginning.

1:26-2:3 What is man?

The sixth day, with the creation of man, was clearly the climax and crowning glory of all God's works. *This* day was 'very good' (31).

Man, in contrast to the Babylonian accounts, where he was made to relieve the gods of the drudgery of work, is given a worthy position. But he remains fundamentally distinct from God: he is not born of God but created. Man is distinguished, however, from the rest of creation, over which he is given the right to rule. Psalm 8 sets out clearly his dependence upon God in this created world. The two passages teach the vital lesson that man, though a creature, is *elevated* by grace into a vital and privileged position of co-operation with God. Our doctrines of man and God are related, and an appreciation of a theology of creation leads to a deeper understanding of ourselves.

Whilst man's authority over the lesser creation is part of his uniqueness in being made in the likeness or image of God (26, 27), there is also a hint of that extra dimension of spirit or soul in man, that capacity for communion with God, which marks him off from the animals. It involves also a capacity for self-determination, i.e. free will. Man was no automaton. There was a danger that man would abuse this trust, but God knew what he was about, and the measure of the risk he took indicates his estimate of the value of fellowship with man of a voluntary and spontaneous kind.

Notes: 1. Due to the Old Testament stress on the sovereignty of God, there is little emphasis on the fact of God as Creator until the period of Amos and Isaiah. *But the truths were already there*, an integral part of Israel's view of the one, supreme God. 2. Whilst *historically* there was no sabbath observance before Moses (Neh. 9:13,14; Ezek. 20:11-13), its *theological* basis is in God's sabbath-rest (2:1-3, compare Exod. 20:11). There is here a divine pattern for man to follow, as well as an awareness of a physical need.

THOUGHT: When man slips from the position occupied here he becomes less than man and little better than the beasts.

2:4-25 Man, and his helper

Some critical scholars regard this section as an alternative, and even contradictory, account of creation, a misrepresentation which does scant justice to the intelligence of the compiler of Genesis. The first two chapters of Genesis, in fact, fulfil different functions. Chapter 1 gives a general picture of creation, cosmic in its extent, and the focus is upon God. In ch.2 the approach is topical and selective, many of the fundamental elements of a complete creation narrative are missing, and man is given greater attention. It is obvious that chs.2 and 3 form a unit (note the title, 'the Lord God' throughout), with 2:15-17 giving essential background information to the account of man's fall. The two creation accounts are complementary, with greater detail given concerning the creation of man and his partner in the second.

The presence of the 'tree of the knowledge of good and evil' (9,17) allowed man the possibility of responsible moral choice in loyal obedience to God's command. We may understand that the fruit of the tree *itself* had no magical quality, but the fruit of obedience or disobedience in man's response to this test was of vital consequence. Was God 'fair' in subjecting man to such a challenge? Would not man have been less than man had there been no test to his will?

Notice the richness of God's provision for man. Food and beauty abounded (9), useful toil was at hand (15) – work *is* a blessing – also gold and precious stones, plus the adventure of discovery, are hinted at in vs.10-14. Eden, the cradle of civilisation, appears to have been located in the Mesopotamian region. God in his loving thoughtfulness also provided a 'helper' fit for man. The Christian doctrine of marriage rests squarely upon this section, especially v.24, where 'leaves' must be understood as a clearly defined break with the former life, i.e. what we understand as a marriage ceremony. Only then do man and his partner become 'one flesh', so this verse provides the most compelling argument against pre-marital sex. Its importance is attested by the number of times in which it is quoted subsequently, and the weight put upon it (e.g. Mark 10:2-9).

TO THINK OVER: Adam and Eve both ate fruit from the forbidden tree (17, compare 3:6) but did not die (physically) in that day (compare 5:5). How are we to understand God's words? Does Rom. 6:23 provide the answer?

3 A subtle foe

Sin, that universal, blighting fact of every generation, is seen in its origins here:

1. Sin – its nature: (*a*) Man, made in the likeness of God, was not basically sinful, but his capacity for the choice of either good or evil involved the possibility of temptation (even Christ was tempted). But Scripture views sin as an intrusion, spoiling something that was essentially good. (*b*) Temptation is personalised as the serpent, who appears as no more than one of the creatures (1). Not until about 200 BC, in the Wisdom literature, was there the specific identification of the personal devil in this incident. But the wiles of the evil one are apparent: (i) he distorts the truth (1b, compare 2,16,17); and (ii) he sows seeds of doubt in man's mind, doubts of God's goodness and integrity, hinting that God is selfishly denying man his right, appealing to man's pride. Throughout history man has bolstered his disobedience and rejection of God by such pseudo-rationalism. The serpent also distorts man's perspective. Multitudinous blessings were to be enjoyed in the garden, but suddenly there was a blind craving for one thing (6). Frail man has often jettisoned the precious relationships of life when dominated by an uncritical fascination for the forbidden.

2. Sin – its effect: (*a*) *Sin seeks to involve others.* Eve involved her husband (6) and blamed the serpent (13). Adam blamed Eve and even God himself, by innuendo (12). (*b*) *Sin cannot be contained.* It involved a generation unborn (16, and the sequel of ch.4) and creation itself (17-19, compare Rom. 8:19-22). (*c*) *It involves self-judgement.* The serpent's promise of opened eyes (5) was fulfilled in a tragically unexpected way – there was an immediate and compelling sense of guilt (7) and they hid themselves (8), long before their exclusion from the garden. Sinful man cannot bear the presence of a holy God (compare Isa. 6:5). Sin separates (compare Isa. 59:1-15).

3. Sin – its vanquisher (15): Evangelical commentators have seen in this dim prophecy the *Protevangelium*, 'the beginning of the gospel'. Certainly it points to the intensity and the costliness of the battle against sin, and the fulfilment in Christ shows just how costly was the undoing of the effects of this chapter in man's redemption.

THOUGHT: 'Where are you (9)?' is God's insistent question after every act of sin. *Where are you* – in relation to your conscience, conversion experience, youthful resolutions, the teaching and standards of home and church, and, above all, in relation to God himself? There is a way back; see 1 John 1:9.

4 The ways divide

This chapter, with its strange mixture of good and evil, is almost prophetic, mirroring in miniature man's subsequent progress. There is much that is unexplained: the identity of those whom Cain feared (14); the origin of his wife (17); and the nature of the sign (15). Sceptics formerly set great store on these; now it is increasingly recognised that Genesis provides a *selective*, not an exhaustive account. Accepting the divine inspiration which underlies selection, it follows that it is wise to concentrate on the *vital* points about which we are actually informed.

The effect of sin becomes increasingly evident in this first family, culminating in the first murder. There is a sad significance in the light of mankind's blood-stained history that it occurred within the family, and in the area of religion. Sacrifice itself is unexplained; it emerges naturally in the God-man relationship. Verses 5-7 (and Heb. 11:4) make it clear that it was Cain's *attitude*, rather than the content of his offering, which made it unacceptable to God. Later legislation (Lev. 2) provided for non-animal sacrifices. We may give according to our individual capacities and, whether it be goods or skills, it is the heart-attitude which God discerns. Cain, like Judas, was shallow; sorry for himself (14) rather than truly repentant. But such was God's unmerited grace that even he was not separated from divine protection (15).

Man's alienation from God is to be understood as *spiritual* and not merely physical (Isa. 59:1-15). So, although we observe the beginning of animal husbandry (20) and the arts (21) and crafts (22), there was also evident that capacity for evil which has frequently misused man's considerable achievements. Lamech's vicious desire for unlimited revenge is perhaps typical (23,24). The Law of Moses brought this under reasonable control (Exod. 21:23-25), but Christ introduced a new dimension (Matt. 18:21,22).

Notes: Verse 1: 'Cain', derived from the verb 'to get', possibly indicates man's acquisitive nature, whilst 'Abel' (2), meaning 'breath', suggests the transience of life. Verse 9: Today's world frequently echoes man's *first*, resentful question, but the Bible is adamant that we have a responsibility to our fellow men. Verse 16: Nod, meaning 'wandering' appears descriptive rather than geographical.

MEDITATION: Two rays of light penetrate (25,26): (*a*) A new beginning in the birth of Seth ('appointed'), hinting at divine intervention through a godly remnant. (*b*) A new attitude – of prayer, with the background of increasing sin and an impelling sense of need.

5 What is life?

The standard commentaries devote minimum space to this the first great genealogical list. Genealogies were of great importance in the ancient world and, whilst they were often selective and occasionally schematic (as in Matt. 1, which omits the names of several unimportant kings), the *invention* of a genealogy was most unlikely. The ten names recorded here invite comparison with the Sumerian King-list, which notes ten kings before the Flood, whose reigns vastly exceed even the large numbers attributed to the patriarchs. Various attempts have been made to reduce the figures in Genesis, by suggesting a different mode of reckoning time (a lunar calendar?), by relating them to a clan rather than to an individual; or by suggesting errors in transmission. All are unsatisfactory. Knowing how atmospheric conditions, stress and other factors influence longevity, the possibility of advanced ages in this early period must be allowed. The general foreshortening of ages may witness to the increasing effect of man's sin. But for the Hebrew, this genealogy is of principal importance because it documents the direct line from Shem (and therefore Adam) to Noah, when a new beginning was made.

Three names stand out: (*a*) *Methuselah* (21-27), the longest-lived man in the Bible. But the comment which comes eight times in this chapter applied to him also . . . 'and he died'. No man is immortal and whilst Methuselah's life was long there was apparently nothing distinctive about it. W. R. Bowie notes, 'His life was long, but thin as a string'. Life can be measured in more ways than one. (*b*) *Enoch* (18-24). His 365 years were vastly more important than Methuselah's immense life-span because he enjoyed a personal relationship with God (24), which put him in the distinguished company of such as Noah, who also walked with God, Abraham, the friend of God, and Moses, whom the Lord knew face to face. The Greek version, which reads 'Enoch pleased God', is saying the same thing in a different way. (*c*) *Lamech* (25-31) made a prophecy based on selfish desire. In fact Noah pronounced *judgement* upon a degenerate world.

Note: Verse 29: 'Noah' is a word play on the verb *nachem*, to comfort or relieve.

MEDITATION: Think about what Psa. 90:4, Rom. 5:14, Heb. 9:27 and Jas. 4:14 teach about life and death. How valid is Ben Sirach's comment, 'In all you do, remember the end of your life, and then you will never sin'?

Questions for further study and discussion on Genesis chapters 1–5

1. 'Genesis ch.1 teaches us as much about the character of God as it does about Creation'. Is this true? What do we learn?

2. What use is made elsewhere in the Old Testament of the doctrine of Creation?

3. How important is Genesis 2 for an understanding of the marriage relationship? What lessons do we learn from it?

4. Consider modern man's total relationship to his environment in the light of the Creation and Fall accounts.

5. In what sense is the Fall individual as well as collective? What evidence can you find for each? What is the role of the Christian in the face of sin in individuals and in the structures of society?

6. What is involved in a 'walk with God' (5:24)? What do we know of it in our own experiences?

6 Man in revolt

In the ancient world there is widespread testimony to a devastating flood, which heightens the historicity of the event. Problems remain concerning: (a) **its timing.** The main Old Testament versions vary in the interval between the Flood and Abraham, from 292 years (Hebrew) via 942 (Samaritan) to 1072 (Septuagint), the latter being the most probable. (b) **Its extent.** The Mesopotamian basin is susceptible to major flooding and the reference *could* be to the total obliteration of a corrupt civilisation in this area. Others would interpret the narrative in universal terms, although the lack of evidence of a major inundation in places such as Asia Minor and Jericho, where there was continual settlement from c.8000 BC onwards, means that the Flood must have occurred *before* that date. Uncertainties of this kind, however, do not disturb the fact itself and the Old Testament account is definite on the main issues:

1. The Flood was an act of judgement. The increasing moral deterioration is clearly documented in vs.5-7, 11-13. Probably vs.1-4 point in the same direction. Interpretations of 'the sons of God' (2) include: (a) fallen angels (compare Job 1:6; Ps. 29:1; Dan. 3:25; 1 Pet. 3:19,20); (b) the line of Seth in contrast to the line of Cain; (c) the descendants of the general creation (Gen. 1) in contrast to the particular (Adamic) creation of Gen. 2; or (d) the high born in contrast to the low born. The second is the most likely alternative; in any case, what happened is regarded as unnatural and blameworthy. The speed at which man, created in the likeness of God (5:1), became corrupted, is depressing. But whenever evil is allowed to enter and control, whenever God is not honoured, both man and society fall into sharp decline. Not only the Flood, but the *total impact* of this ungodliness, must be seen as the judgement of God.

2. There was grace in judgement. Time and time again, in the Old Testament, total, unrelieved judgement was merited (can you think of examples?) but God graciously provided a way of deliverance. Note that he also gave adequate warning. The 120 years (3) probably marks the limit of his forbearance, within which Noah was 'a herald of righteousness' (2 Pet. 2:5) and the ark under construction a vivid visual aid of his prophecy. God's grace through a remnant is one of the great Old Testament truths, but the *size* of that remnant was determined by man's response, not by God's design.

Note: Verse 18: the first mention of 'covenant', although the principle is already involved in 4:15.

7 Judgement falls

The best known Mesopotamian flood account is the Gilgamesh epic. The more recently discovered Atrahasis epic, however, almost a millennium earlier in its extant form, and widely witnessed elsewhere in the ancient Near East, has a closer connection with Genesis in that it includes an account of creation as well as the deluge. It was commonly accepted that Genesis was dependent upon the Mesopotamian accounts, but even amongst critical scholars this view has lost ground to the belief that both accounts are independent versions of a still older tradition. It is recognised that borrowing is not only unproven but unlikely because of the massive revision and reinterpretation involved. A. R. Millard comments, 'If judgement is to be passed as to the priority of one tradition over the other, Genesis inevitably wins for its probability in terms of meteorology, geophysics, and timing alone'. And again, '. . . while the Babylonians could only conceive of the event in their own polytheistic language, the Hebrews, or their ancestors, understood the action of God in it. Who can say it was not so?' (*Tyndale Bulletin*, 1967).

This 'action of God' is stressed in vs.5,9,16, as is the absolute obedience of Noah. The ark was not really a ship, although its dimensions, unlike its Babylonian counterpart, were at least seamanlike. It was simply a huge, three-storeyed raft, with no means of steering or propulsion, i.e. apparently completely at the mercy of the elements. It was so large that it could hardly have been constructed by Noah and his immediate family alone; others shared in its building and its provisioning but despised its shelter, whilst everyone, without exception, who lived in proximity to the completed ark ignored the last week of warning (4, compare 2 Pet. 3:1-10).

Interpretation of some details is difficult, especially the number of animals etc. taken into the ark. 'Seven pairs' (2, etc.) may be interpreted 'by sevens', i.e. three pairs, possibly plus one for sacrifice. The distinction between 'clean' and 'unclean' anticipates the legislation of Lev. 11. Some scholars hold that our author combined two accounts, hence the problem of numbers, but this suggests a clumsy amalgamation which allowed for apparent contradictions. It is preferable to accept the difficulties in our interpretation of facts that were originally clear.

CHALLENGE: 'And Noah did all that the Lord had commanded him' (5, see too vs.9,16)

8 God's care and Noah's faith

Two inter-related themes dominate this chapter.

God's unceasing care and absolute control, the first theme, is involved in the clause 'God remembered Noah'. From the onset of the storm (7:11) to the day of disembarkation covered one year and ten days and imagination should readily convey what it must have felt like, being so helpless and in such apparent danger for so long. To state that God remembered Noah does not infer that he had previously forgotten him, yet it really was a time of trial for Noah as well as a time of judgement on the world. God's promise of vs.21,22, amplified in the covenant of 9:12-17, contains three elements: (*a*) in some measure the curse upon the ground (3:17-19) was modified by Noah's righteous faith, reflected in his sacrifice; (*b*) God declares his future forbearance in the light of man's frailty; (*c*) there will be *no further universal disaster* of such magnitude as to interrupt the sequence of the seasons.

Noah's unfailing faith is the other dominating theme. (*a*) His sending out of the birds vividly depicts the hopefulness of those within the ark; there would be an end to their trial. Presumably the raven did not return (7) because, being an unclean carrion bird, it could survive on the floating carcasses. Not surprisingly, the dove (8) has frequently been seen as a type of the Holy Spirit (compare Matt. 3:16), '. . . sensitive and discriminating, the harbinger of the new creation and the guide of those who await it' (Derek Kidner). Similarly the olive leaf (11), sign of revived vegetation, has become the symbol of peace and pardon, with judgement completed. (*b*) His lack of impatience, resting upon his complete obedience, is shown in the reasonable time allowed between attempts to discover whether the flood had abated, and in waiting for disembarkation instructions (13-17). (*c*) His first act after the deliverance was to sacrifice (20), showing that his thoughts were not selfish but God-ward in gratitude and worship (compare Abraham's similar response in 12:7).

Notes: (*a*) The Babylonian accounts show a marked difference in quality. In the Atrahasis epic the gods, hungry and miserable because their food supply and labour force were affected, regret their action and engage in sharp recriminations. (*b*) Verse 4: *Ararat*. The modern mountain (16,969 ft.) is on the frontiers of Turkey, the USSR and Iran. But the text specifies a region rather than an actual peak, and some scholars suggest a location in the mountainous area north of Mesopotamia.

9 'The everlasting covenant'

A comparison of vs.1-7 with 1:28-30 and 8:17 shows that Noah was viewed as a second Adam, sharing with all creation in a fresh start. But the shadow of man's violence, illustrated in the cases of Cain and Lamech, is seen in the regulations governing the shedding of blood (4-6). Some kind of 'governmental' control is involved in v.6. The attention to the blood anticipates the Mosaic laws and is the background to the New Testament stress on the complete effectiveness of Christ's redeeming blood (e.g. 1 Pet. 1:19). The vital element is that life, symbolised in the blood, belongs to God and is therefore sacred.

The covenant theme dominates Scripture, being contained in the titles, *Old* and *New Testaments* ('covenant' is a preferable translation). The covenant with Noah (8-17) was universal and apparently unconditional since it included the animal creation. No specific stipulations on man's part are defined, unless the general requirements of vs.4-6 are included. The reference to man being made in God's image *could* indicate the need for an attitude and an obedience consistent with this. It may also point to the general knowledge of God and his requirements which can be observed in the natural order as noted in Rom. 1:18-23. The other great biblical covenants are: (*a*) the selective covenant with Abraham (15:17-21), also unconditional, which led on to (*b*) the conditional covenant with Israel through Moses, in which a nation was forged (Exod. 19:1-24:8); (*c*) the covenant with David, in which imagery of the Messiah ultimately displaced an actual reigning king (2 Sam. 7:8-29; Ps. 72) and finally (*d*) the New Covenant (Jer. 31:31-34) fulfilled in Christ (Matt. 26:28; Heb. 8:6-13).

Noah, who 'walked with God' (6:9), was sadly the first recorded drunkard (20-24). The Old Testament strikes a balance, recognising wine as a blessing when rightly used (e.g. Deut. 14:26; Ps. 104:15), but showing a keen awareness of its evil effects when abused (Prov. 23:29-35). Scripture never shrinks from revealing the blemishes of its great saints (compare those of Abraham, Moses, David, Solomon, Elijah, Uzziah and Peter), a witness to the integrity of the record and to the vulnerability of us all unless we maintain the closest relationship with God.

Noah's Song (24-27), like others in the Old Testament (compare 27:27-29,39,40;49:2-27), was a prophecy. Of the descendants of Ham, Canaan (25;10:6) is singled out for special reproach, foreshadowing the intoxication and debauchery associated with the Canaanite fertility-cults. Historically, Canaanites became Israel's slaves when the Conquest was completed.

10 The table of nations

The literary form of this chapter, plus the fact that many of the seventy nations listed here have not been even tentatively identified, suggests that it is indeed an ancient document. The extreme critical view that it was post-exilic, part of the so-called Priestly Code, founders on the fact that no mention is made of Persia, whose benign policies allowed for the restoration of the Jews to their homeland after the exile. Whilst the genealogy of Gen. 5 concentrates on the first-born son, Gen. 10, the second great genealogy, is far more comprehensive. There are remarkably few allusions to historical events. The main purpose served is to bridge the long gap between Noah and the well populated and organised world in which Abraham lived.

'Earth' (32) is usually interpreted as the *known* world, rather than the entire world, since the geographical range is limited by Elam (22) in the East; Sheba (or 'Seba', 7) and 'Cush' (Ethiopia, 6) in the South: Greece and its neighbouring islands in the West (accepting the identification: 'Javan', 2, as Ionia; 'Dodanim', 4, as Rhodes; 'Caphtorim', 14, as the inhabitants of Crete) unless 'Tarshish' (4) refers to Spain or Sardinia, thus taking the boundary further westward; the northern limit seems to be the area of Caucasia, represented by 'Ashkenaz' (3, the Scythians) and 'Gomer' (2, the Cimmerians). Lud appears twice (13,22) and may refer to separate groups, or be a witness to the kind of inter-relationship between the groups which undoubtedly occurred. Generally speaking, the descendants of Shem occupied the middle region between the Japhetic tribes in the North and the Hamitic groups in the South. Since the subsequent history is concerned almost exclusively with the line of Shem, this is dealt with last (21-31), the position of prominence, although Shem was the first-born (5:32). In Shem's family, Eber (21), from which 'Hebrew' derives, was especially important. It is possible that minor modifications were made to this list to cope with emergent groups arising from the established nations. The reference to the Philistines (14) evidences this.

THOUGHT: (*a*) In spite of the immense diversity noted here, all mankind has a common origin, not merely physically, but in the gracious purpose of God (compare 'and his *sons*' – *plural*, in 9:1). (*b*) Verses 8-12. Nimrod, the first great man, the founder of the first, great, self-important and rebellious city (11:1-9). Was there a connection?

11 The scene set

1. Man's rebellious pride (1-9). Although this incident concerns only one migratory group (2), its effects are understood to be universal (9). As the sole post-deluge event in the biblical record before the call of Abraham it is important as typifying man's pride in his achievements. Most scholars accept that some kind of Ziggurat was intended. Archaeology has revealed many examples of these. Pyramidal in shape, and with massive foundations almost as deep as the height of the actual structure, they rose in terraces to the sanctuary. Probably it was a logical combination of a community gathered round a shrine and the high place (originally a hill top), the traditional place of worship. God was thus thought to be contained within the community, but there is always grave danger when the roles are reversed, and man imagines he can control God.

This futile effort, significantly, took place on the site of Babylon. A later king of Babylon also exalted himself in arrogant pride against God but was brought low (Isa. 14:4,12-15), and Rev. 18 depicts the just overthrow of the final corrupt, prosperous, proud and godless civilisation referred to as Babylon. But however great man's achievements God still looks down (5). Man *proudly* builds up in a pathetic desire for immortality ('let us make a name for ourselves', 4) which can never be secured by human effort, but God reached down in *humility* to redeem man, and make him God-like, in Christ. A further contrast is that, whilst human pride must inevitably incur judgement and result in disunity and division, God plans a day when a great multitude 'from all tribes and peoples and tongues' (Rev. 7:9,10) will share in joyous union. Pentecost (Acts 2:5-11) foreshadowed this event.

2. God's careful plan (10-32). This genealogy, externally mundane, documents the final phase before God's redemptive plan took a decisive step forward in the call of Abraham. Acts 7:1-4 makes it clear that God's initial call came to him at Ur, but in a patriarchal society it would have been virtually impossible to journey from Ur to Haran without Terah's consent. In fact, Terah actually accompanied his son on the first long stage to the promised land, although the settlement at Haran (31) *may* have delayed Abraham's further progress.

Note: Verse 9, 'Babel'. Although there is no archaeological evidence for Babylon prior to c.1800 BC, Babylonian tradition, as well as an inscription by the king of neighbouring Agade (c.2250 BC), claiming to have rebuilt the Ziggurat at Babylon, supports its earlier existence.

Questions for further study and discussion on Genesis chapters 6-11

1. Is the state of society today itself a part of God's judgement? What aspects might indicate this? What pointers are there to God's mercy also operating?

2. The ark has often been viewed as a type of the Church. How far is this analogy helpful or applicable?

3. Examine the use made of the Flood narrative elsewhere in Scripture, especially in Peter's Epistles.

4. To what degree can Noah be regarded as a 'second Adam'?

5. What can we learn from Noah about the character of true faith? What incidents in his life seem especially significant?

6. The theologian Eichrodt makes 'covenant' the unifying theme of his 'Theology of the Old Testament'. Can you think of anything more adequate?

7. Is the principle of blood-revenge (9:6) still relevant or has it been superseded in some way? What difference has the coming of Christ made to our attitudes to such areas?

8. 'Man's greatest achievements are frequently the point at which he vaunts himself against God'. Is there any justification for a statement like this?

12 Spotlight on Abraham

Verses 1-4 mark one of the great biblical turning points. Up to this point Genesis has covered briefly, and yet adequately for an understanding of the unfolding drama of divine redemption, the history of thousands of years. Now the remaining chapters are devoted to the four patriarchs.

Patriarchal religion has often been misleadingly described as 'simple'. Granted that the outward forms of prayer and sacrifice (7,8), tithing (14:20), and circumcision (17:23-27) were *relatively* simple, there is much else which fills out the picture. Abraham enjoyed a deep personal acquaintance with God, seldom found elsewhere in the Old Testament, and his faith was so strong that, in response to God's command, it was capable of great sacrifice, as here in his removal from Haran's security to the uncertainty of Canaan. In contrast to the prevailing view of Abraham's day, the power of his God was not limited to a particular territory; wherever he went in his extensive travels, God was there. This is paralleled by another unique feature that was never lost in Israel, an expectant hope. This rested on God's promise (1-3) which concerned a country (the promised land), numerous descendants, and also which, most remarkably, embraced the whole world. Later Judaism often proved insular and unlovely, but throughout true men of God recognised that his saving purposes were universal (compare Isa. 49:6; Mic. 4:1-4). There was a dynamic quality in Abraham's faith.

Scripture, however, reveals honestly the blemishes of even its greatest men. There appears no suggestion in the narrative (10-20) that God directed Abraham to Egypt. The motive seems to have been purely personal – the 'granary of the world' seeming an obvious refuge in a time of famine. Although there was material enrichment (16;13:2) this was evidently an unhappy episode in Abraham's life. Fear of man, accompanied as always in such instances by a lack of trust in God, led to deception and half-truths. Technically, there was truth in Abraham's suggestion (13), for Sarah was his half-sister (20:12). Archaeology has familiarised us with the Hurrian fratriarchal system, which probably applied at Haran. In this a wife, unrelated in any other way, could be legally adopted as a sister in order to establish rights of inheritance and guarantee genealogical purity. But Abraham's action, intended to deceive, was inexcusable. Even the 'father of the faithful', as Abraham is traditionally known, needed to 'watch and pray'.

THOUGHT: Whenever God says 'Go', he always promises, 'I will . . .' (1-3).

The world of the Patriarchs

Black Sea

HITTITE EMPIRE

PADAN

ASSYRIA

Carchemish

Haran

Nineveh

R. Euphrates

Ugarit

R. Tigris

Byblos

Mari

Mediterranean

BABYLONIA

Shechem

Kish

Nippur

Jerusalem

Gerar

Mamre

Erech

Beer-sheba

MOAB

Ur

EDOM

Memphis

EGYPT

MIDIAN

Red Sea

0	100	200miles
0	150	300km

13 Compromise or consecration?

1. The road to restoration. Egypt had been a humbling experience for Abraham, and we are surely to understand that his return to the Bethel area was in the nature of a pilgrimage (3,4), akin to Elijah's return to Horeb (1 Kings 19:8-18). Both men desired a restoration of their fellowship with God. For the Christian our way of returning after backsliding is revealed in 1 John 1:9. Abraham's newly restored fellowship immediately showed itself in: (a) his concern for God's honour (7,8). God's name would be dishonoured in the sight of their neighbours if Lot and he, as 'kinsmen', quarrelled (compare Neh. 5:9); (b) his concern for peace (8,9). How easily the feud between their retainers (7) could have escalated into bitter strife and personal animosity! Yet all the rights were on Abraham's side: the call and the promises were directed exclusively to him, and not to Lot. Moreover, in a patriarchal society his word was law. He could easily have directed Lot to go. Instead, he laid aside his rights and his material interests for the sake of peace. Surely Christ chose his words carefully in Matt. 5:9, for in the role of peacemaker a person becomes most like God.

Note the fulfilment of God's abiding promise to honour those who honour him (1 Sam. 2:30). Hardly had Lot departed than he hastened to confirm the promises already given (14-17). This included in its scope ('eastward', 14) the territory which Lot was moving to occupy. Abraham might lose the companionship of avaricious Lot, but he retained the fellowship of his gracious God.

2. The road to ruin. Lot had made an apparently voluntary good start with Abraham (12:4), but unlike his uncle, he, like many others, could not cope with wealth. Evidently there was a mean, acquisitive streak in him, evidenced by the way in which he selfishly calculated where the best pasture lay. Tragically for him, he failed to weigh the evil influence of notorious Sodom (13). This fatal compromise, as in the cases of Solomon (1 Kings 11:1-8) and Demas (2 Tim. 4:10), proved his undoing. Verse 18 indicates an area about 25 miles south of Jerusalem. Was Abraham moving consciously further away from the place of temptation?

OUR CHOICE: The call of affluence and the easy life is as strong for us as it was for Lot. To yield to it may mean the weakening of our Christian witness. The alternative, if we are to retain our relationship with God, may be a simpler life.

14 Abraham and the wider world

1. The Battle (1-12). Contemporary scholarship views this account of the campaign of four cities against the rebellious five cities in the vicinity of the Dead Sea as originating from the victorious group, since its scope includes minor successes gained against other tribes *en route* (5-7). Its description of the terrain (10) also indicates its antiquity, since this changed abruptly when Sodom and Gomorrah were destroyed (see comments on ch.19). The four 'super-powers' (1) cannot be positively identified, although Tidal bears a strong resemblance to *Tudhalia*, the name of several Hittite kings. It is generally agreed, however, that the names are plausible in the world of that age. This secular record is included solely because Lot was involved (12). No longer did he live outside the city; compromise, as always unless dealt with, had been extended a further step.

2. The Rescue (13-16). Abraham could easily have excused himself from such a dangerous venture by arguing that Lot's plight was self-inflicted; instead he showed a loving, unresentful and sacrificial spirit. Some modern scholars have suggested that his intervention with his armed servants was part of his feudal obligation to the Hittites who then dominated Palestine, but there is no indication of this in the text. Abraham's actions appear motivated by a purely personal concern (14). Notice that Abraham is stated to have been allied to three *Amorite* chieftains, a further mark of authenticity since, in the light of future hostility between Israel and the Amorites, the likelihood of any invention is ruled out.

3. The Aftermath (17-24). (*a*) Abraham recognised in Melchizedek a worshipper of the one, true God and deferred to him as a spiritual superior, receiving his blessing and paying him tithes. The 'bread and wine' (18) probably formed a sacramental meal. Just what influence this godly Canaanite priest-king had upon pre-Israelite Jerusalem cannot be determined, but the suffix *zedek* ('righteousness') persisted in Jerusalem, as in Adoni-zedek (Josh. 10:3) and, *possibly*, Zadok, David and Solomon's priest. (*b*) Abraham had no such respect for the king of corrupt Sodom, and maintained his integrity and independence by refusing his patronage (22-24) without forcing his principles upon his allies (24). The policy of the Jews in accepting the lavish support of a friendly-disposed and humane Persia (Ezra 1) warns us against extracting a *universal* principle from Abraham's policy.

15 Promise and prophecy

The covenant with Abraham, the second of the great biblical covenants (compare 9:8-17), is here introduced without conditions on Abraham's part, thus underlining God's grace (but note ch.17). Unlike the universal covenant with Noah it was *particular*, involving only Abraham and his descendants, although its world-wide implications are noted in 12:3. The promises, developing those already given, were fourfold:

1. Protection (1). The attribute which God here assumes in a close personal relationship, 'the shield of Abraham', is paralleled in contemporary inscriptions and further demonstrates the historicity of the patriarchal narratives. The man who had shielded Lot (14:13-16) was now assured of divine protection.

2. Prosperity (1). Unlike Lot, Abraham was not grasping (compare 14:21-23) but willing to forgo material advantage when principles were at stake. God is no man's debtor; the richest rewards for Abraham were surely worked out in the spiritual realm.

3. An heir (2-6). The Hurrian practice in the case of a barren marriage was, as here, to adopt formally a trusted servant as heir. Probably Eliezer was the faithful retainer of 24:2. Abraham accepted that he would become a father, although his later conduct betrays uncertainty as to the mother (ch.16). This implicit trust in God, in a seemingly impossible situation (6), became the basis of the New Testament view of Abraham's justification by faith (Rom. 4:3,9,22; Gal. 3:6; compare Jas. 2:23).

4. A country (18-21) extending from the Wadi el-Arish ('the river of Egypt'), north-east of Egypt, to the Euphrates. Because of Israel's subsequent unbelief and lack of endeavour, the conquest was not completed until the time of David and Solomon, and even then sections were incorporated by treaty, e.g. Tyre (e.g. 2 Sam. 5:11,12; 1 Kings 5:12) and Hamath (2 Sam. 8:9,10).

The covenant itself was sealed in the most solemn manner known to the ancient world (9-11,17), the two parties passing between the severed portions of the sacrifice signifying the fate of the one who broke his agreement. It was unhurried, occupying possibly a whole day (compare vs.5 and 17).

There was also a prophecy concerning the oppression in Egypt (13), where Israel would experience testing difficulties and delays. Exod. 12:40 gives the *precise* length (compare Acts 7:6). God's future judgement was also foretold against the Egyptians (14) and the Amorites (16), here signifying *all* the inhabitants of the promised land. Note especially God's long-suffering reflected in v.16, indicating his watchfulness over all nations, and showing that Israel's conquest of Canaan was part of his universal moral government.

Abraham in Canaan

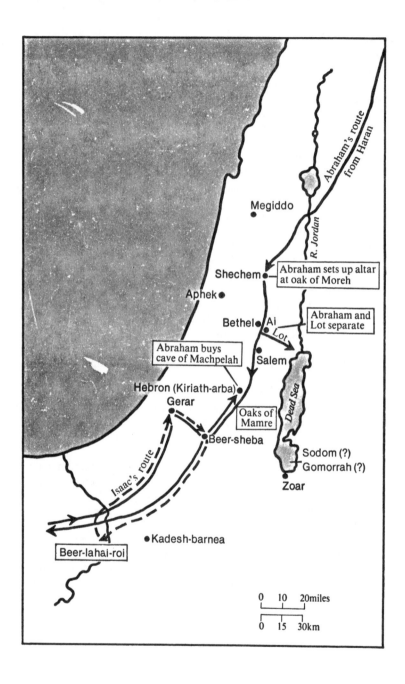

Megiddo

Shechem ●
Abraham sets up altar
at oak of Moreh

Aphek ●

Bethel ● ● Ai
Abraham and
Lot separate
Lot

Abraham buys
cave of Machpelah
Salem

Hebron (Kiriath-arba) ●

Gerar ●
Oaks of
Mamre
● Beer-sheba

Isaac's route

Sodom (?)
Gomorrah (?)
Zoar

Dead Sea

*Abraham's route
from Haran*

R. Jordan

● Kadesh-barnea

Beer-lahai-roi

| 0 | 10 | 20miles |

| 0 | 15 | 30km |

16 'Thy way, not mine'

1. Man's interference (1-6). There is widespread witness in the world of Abraham's time to this practice when a marriage was childless, whereby the wife's maid-servant was given to the husband (compare 30:3). Any child from this union was reckoned as the legitimate heir. Doubtless Sarah's intention was to help forward God's clearly stated plan, and every year that passed would seem to compound an already-impossible situation. What God promises, however, he will fulfil in his own time and manner, and ten years (3) was as nothing to an eternal God (compare Psa. 90:2). Certainly Sarah's impetuous interference, condoned by Abraham, ushered in a saga of trouble and a sequence of unhappiness which has not yet ended. Hagar's contempt (4) provoked Sarah's jealous retaliation which Abraham, strangely spineless, made no effort to counter (5,6). On the wider scale, there is the tragic, long-standing feud between Ishmael's descendants and Israel. This whole incident is viewed by Paul as an allegory contrasting the fruit of human effort (bondage) and the freedom of the Spirit-born (Gal. 4:21-31). Incidentally, the closing verses of the chapter (15,16) show that Abraham did finally accept his responsibility.

2. God's intervention (7-14). Although Abraham's action was not part of his plan, God's fatherly compassion still reached out to Hagar, who, as the place-names show (14), was well on the way to her native Egypt. To return to Sarah and submit was no easy decision, and the Lord's gracious intervention and promise weighed decisively with her. It would be a worth-while exercise to make a note of all the names of God revealed in Genesis, because each one reflects an actual living experience. To 'God hears' (*Ishmael*, 11) was added 'the living one who sees me' (*Beer-lahai-roi*, 14). Her awareness of such a living, responsive and perceptive God provoked deep wonder. How much greater should be the reaction of the Christian who rejoices in 'the light of the knowledge of the glory of God *in the face of Christ*' (2 Cor. 4:6), for 'in him *all the fullness of God* was pleased to dwell' (Col. 1:19)!

Note: In verse 12 'wild ass of a man' typifies the free, unpredictable and bold spirit so characteristic of the nomadic Arab tribes. 'He shall dwell over against all his kinsmen' aptly suggests alienation and opposition.

FOR WORSHIP: Our reaction of wonder to a living, responsive and perceptive God.

17 God's way defined

Abraham's faith was tested over a considerable period, for another thirteen years had slipped past since Ishmael's birth (1, compare 16:16). Now the covenant already made (ch.15) comes into clearer focus. On the God-ward side there is a threefold promise:

(1) Many descendants (4-6). The stress on 'a multitude of nations' shows that the offspring of Ishmael, and probably Esau (Gen. 36), were included (compare v.20).

(2) The land of Canaan (8).

(3) A personal, covenantal relationship (4,7,8). The movement is from the covenant with Abraham to its consummation in the covenant, through Moses, with the whole nation. The application here is twofold: (a) God will be the sole object of Israel's worship and trust; (b) he, as 'God Almighty' (1, Heb. *El Shaddai*, the precise meaning of which is uncertain) will watch over, direct, provide for and fulfil his promises to his people. The absence of the customary 'and they shall be my people' (compare Jer. 7:23; Ezek. 11:20) after 'I will be their God' (8) possibly emphasises that the full initiative is God's, not man's.

There are conditions, however, to the covenant:

(a) 'Walk before me and be blameless' (1). This involves both the enjoyment of the Lord's favour *and* the gaining of his approval by a life of complete moral integrity, a point equally involved in Mic. 6:8 and 1 John 1:7.

(b) Obedience. God here introduces the covenant sign of circumcision (9-14). This was widely practised among the peoples of the ancient world, including the Egyptians and most Semitic peoples apart from the Assyrians, Babylonians and a few isolated groups, e.g. the men of Shechem (Gen. 34). The frequency of the reference to the Philistines as 'uncircumcised' suggests that they were a notable exception to the general rule (e.g. 2 Sam. 1:20). Israel was to be unique, however, in practising the rite in infancy (12). Usually it took place at puberty, which made it of primarily social importance, marking the arrival at the age of manhood, possibly in connection with the fertility cults. By Jeremiah's time this distinctive covenant sign had acquired a corresponding spiritual significance (Jer. 4:4;9:25,26). Note Abraham's immediate obedience (22-27), itself an example of the attitude required.

The fulfilment of the covenant was now precisely defined (15-21). It was not to be by Eliezer (15:2), or even Ishmael, for whom Abraham cherished such prayerful ambitions (18), but Isaac. God's way, even when tested by long delay, is always better than man's cherished but ill-founded plans, and worth waiting for.

Questions for further study and discussion on Genesis chapters 12-17

1. To what extent has the prophecy of Gen. 12:3 been fulfilled? What part do Christians have to play in its fulfilment?

2. 'For every ten persons who can stand the test of adversity only one can stand the test of prosperity'. Does your observation confirm or refute this comment? What are the advantages, and what the dangers of affluence?

3. Is it always wrong for a Christian to move into a situation where the temptations are greatest?

4. Consider the morality of Abraham's actions in (a) taking up arms to rescue Lot and (b) refusing the generous offer of the king of Sodom. What lessons can we find for ourselves?

5. If God is both sovereign and righteous, how does this work out in his judgements in today's world (compare 15:14-16)?

6. Why do we so easily interfere with God's plans for our lives? How can we guard against this?

7. On the basis of the biblical teaching concerning circumcision, think about the relationship of an outward sign to its inward reality. Should the modern Christian have a distinguishing mark of any kind?

18 'Abraham, my friend'

Verses 1-8. Hebrews 13:2 speaks of entertaining angels unawares, but here the revelation was of God himself (1). Abraham was, of course, unaware of the nature of his guests, but like Gideon (Judg. 6:19), and Samson's parents (Judg. 13:15), he was prepared to extend leisurely, personal and sacrificial hospitality which may shame our current, conventional attitude to visitors. Matt. 25:34-46 is a reminder that God can still draw near to us in unrecognisable forms of need, and that how we treat others reflects our relationship with him.

Verses 9-15. The promise had already been given, probably three months before (10, compare 17:17-21). Clearly Sarah had not accepted this earlier word, and her laughter here was prompted by incredulity, based on her physical condition (12). She *knew* that it was impossible for her to bear a child, but she was *wrong* (see Luke 18:27)! The play on the word 'laughter' (compare 17:17) seems to reflect God's tender understanding of her doubts. Later on, Sarah herself, realising the happiness of fulfilment, further developed the pun (21:6).

Verses 16-33. Communication with God is not merely a one-way transaction, in which we only present our needs. He delights to share his mind and will with us; in the communion of prayerful fellowship we, like Abraham, are permitted to question and explore his will. There may be times when, because of our imperfect understanding, we find it difficult to reconcile our notions of God's character with his actions. In such instances it is best to take our doubts directly to him in prayer, as did Jeremiah (Jer. 12:1-6) and Habakkuk (Hab. 1:13). Abraham was certain that God would not do anything inconsistent with his character of perfect love and righteousness (25). We may pray in the confidence that he is never arbitrary, hasty or vindictive.

An omniscient God would know all along the pathetically small number of the righteous in Sodom and would be deeply concerned for them. All the same, Abraham's prayer remains a model of humble, persistent intercession motivated by a concern for people. The gradual reduction in numbers may reflect Abraham's fears concerning the extent of Lot's influence in Sodom, but he over-estimated this by stopping at ten (32). In fact Lot's testimony was so ineffective that only four, from his immediate family, were saved (19:16).

QUESTION: How do we hear God speaking to us today?

19 Lot's tragic end

Isaiah 1:9;13:19; Jer. 49:18 and Ezek. 16:46-58 show the profound effect on Israel of the judgement of Sodom and Gomorrah – God's judgement *must* fall when evil has reached such proportions. Note that the Sodomites' lust was in no way deterred by their supernatural blindness (11, an unusual word, suggesting that they were dazzled).

The chapter documents the tragic decline of Lot, whose good qualities are evident. His compelling offer of hospitality (3) was doubtless motivated by his knowledge of the city's evil reputation, but he was certainly concerned and courageous (6). In the ancient world protection was a vital part of hospitality. Lot's initial compromise in moving to the vicinity of Sodom had now escalated to the point where he was confronted with two vicious alternatives, and in an age when unmarried daughters were considered the property of their fathers, he was the readier to sacrifice (the incident in Judg. 19:22-30 illustrates this) his daughters rather than his guests. He appears as a pathetic figure, although now a ruler, as v.1 indicates. The men of Sodom regarded him as an upstart (9); his intended sons-in-law treated him as a joke (14).

Lot seemed curiously reluctant to leave Sodom in spite of urgent appeals and, eventually, physical constraint (15-20). Possibly he regretted the loss of his possessions; possibly he lacked faith in God's willingness to provide for him in the future; possibly it was shame which prevented him from taking the obvious but humiliating course of rejoining Abraham. His fearful conduct (19,30) betokens a man who has lost effective touch with God. In this crisis the intercessory prayer of Abraham (27-29) seems to have been the decisive influence. The fate which overtook his wife and daughters is a reminder that, when we put ourselves in the place of danger and temptation, we inevitably expose our dependants, who may be more vulnerable.

Archaeology evidences a significant break in the occupation of this area which appears to connect with this incident. Possibly Sodom and Gomorrah were in an area now covered by the south-east part of the Dead Sea.

Notes: Verse 1: the third 'angel', the Lord himself, had remained with Abraham (18:22). Verse 26: Lot's wife, engulfed in the catastrophe, is symbolic of all who turn back (Luke 17:31,32).

20 A prophet shamed

A critical approach to Genesis has frequently suggested that this section is merely a duplicate of 12:10-20, or possibly even a triplicate, if 26:6-11 is taken into consideration. In each chapter, however, there are distinctive elements, and experience illustrates the undeniable fact that we do tend to repeat our mistakes, failing to profit from them, especially when fear, or another equally strong emotion, is involved. Fear cripples, and even a godly man like Abraham acted completely out of character, without regard for Sarah or Abimelech. He even jeopardised God's promise by his apparent willingness to surrender Sarah (2). Verse 13 seems to imply that Abraham had lived under the constant shadow of fear, which if it truly reflects a timid spirit, makes his ventures of faith the more remarkable.

There is further realism in this picture of Abraham's lapse when compared with the preceding chapter, with its reminder of him as a spiritual prayer-giant, vitally involved in God's deliverance of Lot (19:27-29). Few are able to live a life of sustained spiritual triumph; most of us suffer those humiliating valley experiences of failure following swiftly after times of spiritual exaltation. However, this is *not* unavoidable; God has provided adequately for a life of sustained fellowship with himself. Here he is seen at work, rescuing Abraham from his self-inflicted predicament as earlier he had delivered Lot. One feels a sympathy for Abimelech, a heathen king behaving in a remarkably upright and forthright manner, apparently more sinned against than sinning. Evidently God had regard to this, delivering him and his dependants from the consequences of his action. In this, Abraham's prayers again played a major part (7,17), reminding us that a sinner restored by God's grace can immediately resume the ministry of intercessory prayer.

Note: Verse 7: 'prophet'. The derivation suggests an original meaning of 'ecstatic', but, as used in the Old Testament, it refers to God's spokesman and accredited representative. Some Old Testament prophets appear as ecstatics. A comparison of the relationship between Moses and Aaron is revealing – see Exod. 4:15-17;7:1,2.

QUESTION: Can we reason from v.6 that sexual impurity is still an offence against God himself?

21 Strained relationships

Agur's declaration that, 'Every word of God proves true' (Prov. 30:5) is illustrated here. God's promise to Abraham was fulfilled in his own way and perfect time (1,2), in spite of its seeming impossibility (7). The pun on Isaac's name (compare 17:17; 18:12-15) is sustained in this joyous passage (6) with a possible inference that Sarah herself would be the target of much derision. This may have been the factor which goaded her when Ishmael mocked Isaac (9, RSV 'playing', compare Gal. 4:29), who at the time of his weaning would be about three years old. Tension was bound to arise in such a situation. Years before, Abraham, encouraged by Sarah, had 'sown to the flesh' in attempting to work out God's promise (16:1-4). Now he discovered the harsh reality that, 'Whatever a man sows, that he will also reap' (Gal. 6:7). The culmination, in the expulsion of Hagar and her son, was inevitable. Abraham's reluctance was probably a combination of his natural affection, and the contemporary law that if a genuine heir was born after the adoption of a substitute, the latter was not to be discriminated against. Although Abraham was no longer within the jurisdiction of the Mesopotamian cities, where this custom prevailed, he doubtless felt its strength, not acting until he received a direct word from God (12,13). As in the earlier incident (16:7-14), the agony of an outcast mother did not escape God (15-21), nor was he unmindful of his promise (17:20).

The relationship between Abraham and Abimelech (22-34) demonstrates that affairs between comparative strangers can be conducted courteously, honourably and peaceably. The type of agreement noted here is known as a parity covenant. Normally made between equals, it seems that in this case Abimelech's superiority in physical resources was offset by his awareness that God was with Abraham (22). Abraham, settled in the land by favour of Abimelech (20:15), would welcome a guaranteed, cordial relationship. In an immediate test-case, concerning ownership of a well, friction was avoided by a continued display of brotherliness. Abimelech's acceptance of Abraham's seven ewes (30) would confirm the latter's right to the well. This incident, featuring a warm relationship between a Philistine and the chief Hebrew patriarch, is *not* likely to have been invented later, when the Philistines were Israel's inveterate enemies.

Note. Verse 31: Beer-sheba is a double pun, 'well of seven' (referring to the seven ewes) and, in a secondary sense, 'well of the oath'.

22 God will provide

Abraham's position as the 'father of the faithful' was gained through frequent testing and challenge. Already he had surrendered the *past* in the clear break with Ur and Haran (11:31-12:4), to which he never returned. He had surrendered *present* advantage when he allowed Lot the choice of the most favourable pasture (13:8-12). These tests, however, appear almost insignificant when compared with the challenge to sacrifice Isaac, for the fulfilment of God's future promises seemed inextricably bound up in the boy. There may have been an added poignancy for Abraham in that he had surrendered his personal desire for fulfilment through Ishmael, in obedience to God's word concerning Isaac (17:18-21). Any prospect of a further heir through Sarah must have appeared incredibly remote. How could he reconcile God's former promises and this stark command, with himself cast as the executioner (2)?

But Abraham's faith never wavered. God had given Isaac, and it was his prerogative to take him away should he desire this (see Job 1:21). Abraham did not question nor procrastinate, and the bundle of firewood (3) amply demonstrates his total obedience. He knew that the future could be safely entrusted to God. Hebrews 11:19 states clearly that Abraham envisaged a resurrection, which is the more remarkable in that the next *clear* reference to a resurrection came over one thousand years later (Isa. 26:19).

Abraham's confidence in God's provision of a substitute sacrifice (8) was amply justified (13). Since 2 Chron. 3:1 identifies Moriah (2) as the site of Solomon's Temple and since, at adjacent Calvary, God 'did not spare his own Son but gave him up for us all' (Rom. 8:32), there is an almost prophetic element in Isaac's wondering question '. . . where is the lamb . . . ?' (7). Theologically, this was answered ultimately by John the Baptist's ringing declaration 'Behold, the Lamb of God' (John 1:29; compare 1 Pet. 1:18-21).

Our awareness that God knew the end from the beginning does not detract from the magnificence of Abraham's faith. This severe test was rewarded by a richer renewal of the promise (15-18). Possibly, in a world where the first-born son was sometimes sacrificed, God was demonstrating his abhorrence of child sacrifice and yet, at the same time, underlining his sovereign claim upon the first-born (Num. 3:11-13).

Note: Verses 20-24. The family of Nahor (compare 11:27-29) is introduced at this point in anticipation of ch.24. *Rebekah* is the focal point of interest (23).

Questions for further study and discussion on Genesis chapters 18-22

1. What is the Christian's obligation to hospitality? Why are we so reluctant to offer it?

2. What is the relationship between our prayer and the sovereign will of God?

3. Does God always work to preserve his servants from the effects of their own folly?

4. Is it possible to stand alone in a hostile and evil environment? What qualities does it require that Lot may have lacked? What should the Christian attitude be to possible involvement in such situations?

5. Think about Lot's compromising spirit in the light of the attitude of Joseph and Daniel.

6. 'God is with you in all that you do' (21:22). How can we demonstrate this in today's world?

7. Which has first priority – personal ambition or our plans for our children? Which do you find it easier to sacrifice? Why?

8. List the different ways in which Abraham is an example and a warning to us.

23 The valley of the shadow

Modern scholarship finds this a fascinating chapter because of its close relationship to conditions and customs prevalent in the Hittite Empire which, centred in eastern Asia Minor, extended its influence as far south as Kiriath-arba (possibly renamed Hebron after its capture by Israel, Judg. 1:10). This detailed record of an estate transaction, with particular reference to the *place* (10, the gate of a city, being the most convenient and possibly only open space, was the obvious centre for civic and commercial matters), the *witnesses* (7,10,12,13 etc.) and the *form* (17-20, the special mention of trees is a feature of Hittite records) can be paralleled in contemporary documents. Indeed, our increasing knowledge of conditions in the ancient Near East reveals a consistency with Genesis which makes scepticism unrealistic. Another seemingly incidental yet important matter is the way in which Israel's patriarchal fathers are depicted – here Abraham confesses that he was 'a stranger and a sojourner' (4). This is hardly likely to have been invented in a later age when the patriarchs were revered. One less convincing suggestion is that, since under Hittite law Abraham would possibly be responsible for Ephron's feudal obligations had he purchased *all* the latter's property, Abraham, by seeking to secure the cave only (9), was trying to escape these requirements. Since we do not know whether all Ephron's property was involved there can be no finality on this point. The actual transaction reveals typical oriental courtesy masking what was probably a hard bargain – 400 shekels seems a very steep price (16), but Abraham was not in the mood or position to haggle. There is pathos in the fact that the man who possessed divine rights to the title deeds of the whole land (13:14-18) actually owned only a dearly-bought burial site (compare Acts 7:5).

This human aspect makes Abraham, that giant of faith, like the rest of us who share his humanity and who, like him, experience bereavement. Imagine his heartache during this period of wrangling. Sarah, who had shared his joys and sorrows, hopes and fears, successes and failures – his very life – was dead. The name of God occurs nowhere in this chapter, but 24:1, which notes 'the Lord had blessed Abraham *in all things*' (compare Rom. 8:28) surely does not exclude this sad chapter. The constant companionship of his *friend* must have been especially precious during these sad days. We, as Christians, have an equally rich heritage (compare Matt. 28:20; 2 Tim. 4:17; Heb. 13: 5-8).

24:1-33 The ideal servant

It may seem strange that the longest chapter in Genesis should be minutely concerned with a love story. The detail is strange to the conventions of the western world, but there is nothing trivial in the outworking of God's will. Abraham, aware of the need for purity in the chosen line, and perhaps mindful of Ishmael's mixed marriage (21:21; compare Esau's action in 26:34), was resolute on this main issue (6-8), convinced that God would be true to him.

He also demonstrates complete faith in his servant, to whom this delicate mission was entrusted, and he was not disappointed. Since the focus is on the *servant*, note: (*a*) If he is to be identified with Eliezer (15:2) then, like John the Baptist in relation to Christ (John 3:30), he was a truly selfless man. Superseded as heir by Isaac, he was still content to serve Abraham faithfully. (*b*) Before he set out, he made sure of the details of his commission (5-9), an example to all who are called to the Lord's work (compare Acts 22:10). (*c*) Whilst he was clearly free to make full use of Abraham's resources, so that he could represent his master worthily (10, see Matt. 28:18; 2 Cor. 9:8), there was no ostentation or extravagance. (*d*) He surrounded the mission with prayer (12) which was personal, even though the language emphasises his place within the family of which Abraham was head. (*e*) In seeking to test God's will he proposed a practical test which would amply demonstrate Rebekah's character (13,14). To draw water willingly for ten thirsty camels required a kind heart and a capacity for hard work. (*f*) Although the outcome seemed clear (18-20) he did not jump to hasty conclusions (21), as Joshua and his elders did when confronted with the Gibeonites (Josh. 9:3-15). It is fatally easy to rush into what may seem to be God's obvious will. In this case, however, confirmation was soon forthcoming (24). (*g*) Without any self-congratulation on the apparently successful outcome, he thanked God for answered prayer (26,27). God's servants have not always been able to avoid deflecting the glory that is properly his on to themselves. (*h*) In contrast with the normal pace of Eastern etiquette there was a sense of urgency in his mission (33), with his own comfort secondary to his master's business.

Notes: Verse 2, 'thigh' (compare 47:29), the personal area of procreation, witnessing to a particularly sacred oath. Verse 10, 'the city of Nahor', i.e. where Nahor lived, possibly Haran.

THOUGHT: God's servants have not always been able to avoid deflecting the glory that is properly his on to themselves.

24:34-67 Mission completed

Our modern techniques in the printing and production of books allow for a flexibility unknown in the ancient world. A book like Genesis was probably about the maximum possible length, beyond which a scroll would become unwieldy and impossibly heavy, a fact which made careful selection a necessity. Therefore, wherever we find recapitulation of a major kind (as in vs.37-48), we do well to seek the reason (compare the reduplication in Acts chs.10;11, where the vital extension of the gospel to a Roman centurion was involved, or the crucial importance of Christ's encounter with Paul in the testimonies of Acts chs.22;26). The emphasis here is on the out-working of God's will in such clarity that Laban can only admit, 'The thing comes from the Lord . . .' (50). It is one of the principles of the Old Testament faith that *God speaks through events* (as here), which is partly the reason why what we term 'historical books' (Joshua, Judges, Samuel and Kings) are included amongst 'The Former Prophets' in the Hebrew canon. It was apparent that the God who had so signally blessed Abraham (35) had also directed and prospered the way of his servant (27,56). Following the previous comments, we may also note Eliezer's clear testimony, his lack of procrastination (56; contrast the prophet from Judah who was waylaid by the old prophet from Bethel, 1 Kings 13), and the way in which, his task completed, he retired unobtrusively from the scene (compare Luke 17:7-10). In the light of Laban's subsequent treatment of Jacob (chs.29-31), vs.30-32 probably reveal his calculating, avaricious spirit. Since Bethuel, the father of Laban and Rebekah, figures only incidentally (50), it is likely that he was so old that his eldest son bore the responsibility for the marriage arrangements.

Notes: Verse 59: Rebekah's nurse, Deborah (35.8), remained a faithful family servant well into the next generation. Verse 64: it was a mark of respect to dismount in the presence of a person of rank. Verse 65: 'It is my master' (compare v.34). Isaac is accepted as the heir, the reference marking a transition away from the aged Abraham.

FOR WORSHIP AND THANKSGIVING: Consider the ways in which God has led you.

25 Family details

A comparison of 21:5 and 25:7,20 shows that Abraham lived for thirty-five years after Isaac's marriage, so that his grandsons would be fifteen years old when he died (26). Abraham's prime concern was to safeguard the interests of Isaac, the child of promise (5,6). His sentimental attachment to Ishmael, however, still remained, with the lines of communication open, so that Ishmael was able to participate in the funeral arrangements (9). In the next generation two other strangely diverse brothers were brought together in their father's death (35:29).

Following Abraham's death, Isaac might have been expected to dominate, but he appears as a mild, contemplative type (24:63). Sandwiched as he was between a great father and an equally notable son, he is almost passed over in the catalogue of the patriarchs. Even so, God was with him (11). In this chapter the interest is more in the rivalry between his two sons. As the prophetic oracle indicated, Rebekah was the mother of two nations (23) whose hostility appeared to increase rather than diminish throughout the Old Testament period. A few minutes with a concordance would illustrate the prophets' condemnation of Edom's (the nation descended from Esau) unbrotherly attitude to Israel. There is a double play in v.25: 'red' connects with Edom; 'hairy' connects with Mt. Seir, Edom's traditional stronghold (33:16).

The different natures of the two sons soon became apparent. Esau was the more virile, extrovert and probably more attractive superficially. Jacob was the quieter, 'stay at home' type. His name probably means 'May God protect you', but with the possible alternative of the 'One who supplants' (26, see RSV margin). In fact, it was the latter which became characteristic, as Esau was to comment bitterly (27:36). In vs.33,34 there is already evidence of an unscrupulous, scheming nature divorced from any semblance of brotherliness. But at least Jacob showed an appreciation of higher values. The birthright involved spiritual privileges and responsibilities within the family as well as material benefits (Deut. 21:17). In the circles in which the patriarchs originated it was a relationship which could be purchased and so transferred, but never for anything as trivial as a bowl of pottage (compare Heb. 12:16).

Each son had a champion (28), and so the seeds of future family discord were sown.

QUESTION: How can parents overcome natural affinities and prejudices and so guard against favouritism?

26 'Blessed are the peacemakers'

The theme of God's faithfulness and man's fallibility continues in vs.1-16. Isaac was challenged to rely on God's provision in a time of famine, rather than on the material certainty of Egypt, the granary of the world. Although God's blessing upon Isaac is noted in 25:11, this was apparently the first direct encounter (2-5), and like the second one (23-25), it was associated with a time of trial. In both instances, the continuity of God's covenantal blessings was renewed in this second generation. The critical tendency to regard vs.6-11 as a confused account of the similar incidents concerning Abraham (12:10-20;20) is, as we have already noted, unwarranted. The differences in detail are considerable: 26:1 shows an awareness of the first offence; and Abimelech's prompt reaction (9-11) suggests his painful recollection of an earlier event. Although Isaac was not born until after his father's two lapses he doubtless knew about them. In his case too fear of man proved his undoing. No attempt is made to cover up the blemishes of these pioneer patriarchs. There is encouragement for us in that the Lord continues patiently with such fallible material.

Note that Isaac began a new phase of sedentary occupation (12) which involved a greater dependence on an assured local water supply, hence the vital nature of the arguments over wells which dominates vs.17-33. Although eclipsed by both Abraham and Jacob, Isaac appears here in a praiseworthy role. The wearisome disputes with the men of Gerar could easily have escalated into a major incident. But Isaac, refusing to be provoked, kept moving (and digging!) until his right was undisputed (22), and so became the first peacemaker of the Bible (see also Prov. 15:1; Matt. 5:9; 2 Tim. 2:24).

Abimelech and Phicol (26-31) are not necessarily to be identified with the Philistines of the same name in 21:22-32. The names could be those of officials, or family names, which frequently tend to alternate in the generations of a family in the ancient world, so that a son would have the name of his grandfather. Nor is the incident concerning Beersheba (23-25,32,33) a duplicate of the earlier incident (21:32). Abraham's well may have been re-opened (15,23-25) or it may have been an entirely new well, in either case the new experience would give fresh significance to the old name.

QUESTION: Why did Esau's action make life bitter for Isaac (compare 24:3)?

27 Man proposes, God disposes

In the ancient world the patriarchal blessing was of great importance, especially if given near the point of death, as Isaac considered himself to be, although in fact he lived a further forty years (35:27-29). It was legally binding, and was also a type of prophecy with an inherent power of fulfilment. This sad chapter, from which no one emerges with credit, is altogether devoid of such family qualities as mutual trust, the honouring of vows, and loving care. When read against the background of 25:29-34 it must be assumed that every member of the family knew that Esau had, by a vow, traded away his birthright (compare Heb. 12:16,17).

Isaac's blatant preference for Esau was undoubtedly a major factor in causing these events: this despite his awareness of the promise, 'the elder shall serve the younger' (25:23), and that Esau had compromised his position further by mixed marriages (26:34,35). This amounted to wilful disobedience to God. Isaac appears as a gluttonous, self-indulgent man. His one redeeming feature is that, realising that he had been outwitted by Jacob, and overruled by God, he immediately accepted that the irreversible blessing had been given to the right person (33,37). Rebekah, the shrewd 'brain' of the family, was also guilty of favouritism, possibly as a corrective to the Isaac/Esau relationship. Her suspicions of her husband are evident as, with an almost diabolical cunning which covered every contingency, she engineered events. When Esau's attitude threatened Jacob's life (41) she again acted with insight, knowing that Esau was incapable of harbouring permanent resentment (45). In fact, twenty years elapsed before Jacob's return, during which he was tormented by nightmares of his brother's vengeance. Deceit and intrigue left, as always, a legacy of division and fear.

Jacob, an adept accomplice, carried out the deception without a qualm, compounding lie upon lie (19,24), and adding the most blatant hypocrisy (20). A natural sympathy for Esau, completely out-smarted by this wily alliance, must not be blind to the fact that he *knew* that he had lightly squandered his privileges. At least, however, he was transparent enough to be incapable of keeping his murderous feelings to himself (41). But there was a long-standing legacy, itself a fulfilment of v.40, in the subsequent hostility between the Israelites and Edomites (see 2 Sam. 8:13,14; 2 Kings 8:20-22).

QUESTION: How could God work his will through this web of intrigue?

28 God is revealed to Jacob

Isaac, now reconciled to the fact that God's chosen line included Jacob, not Esau, made provision for the future by sending Jacob away, with his unqualified blessing, to find an approved wife (1-5). This prompted Esau to action, but his marriage to his cousin seems a clumsy attempt to make amends (6-9, see 26:34,35;27:46).

Probably on the second night Jacob reached the vicinity of Luz (v.19 clearly distinguishes 'that place' from 'the city'). There would be a heathen sanctuary at Luz, but Jacob's tiny 'shrine' where he, apparently for the first time, encountered God personally, would in no way be compromised by this association. The 'ladder' (12) was a vivid reminder that there was no unbridgeable gulf between heaven and earth; God was constantly, protectively in contact. Such a revelation was evidently a new discovery, for Jacob appears surprised to find God away from the sanctuaries associated with his father. It was common in the ancient world to think of a god's authority and power as limited to a particular national territory. Such a belief is far from the thought of this chapter. God's power, Jacob discovered, was universal. God promised his presence and protection *wherever* Jacob went, and his plan was certain of fulfilment (15). So the 'covenant with Abraham' was renewed in this third generation (13-15). Jacob, however, remained the bargainer (18-22), somewhat lacking in faith and rather preoccupied with self and material interests. God's assurance 'I will' (15) prompted only the tentative response of 'If' (20). 'Me' and 'I' occur frequently in his words, and his vow of a tenth seems poor recompense in the light of God's unlimited benefits to him. Jacob still had a long way to go on his spiritual pilgrimage, but at least he had made a promising start.

Notes: Verse 19. 'Bethel', ten miles north of Jerusalem, and already associated with Abraham (12:8), became the central shrine for some time during the Judges period (Judg. 20:18,26). When the kingdom divided after Solomon's death, Jeroboam I made it the principal shrine for the northern tribes (1 Kings 12:26-33). Later it came under the strong condemnation of Amos (Amos 3:14;4:4;5:4-7). Verse 22, 'the tenth'. The principle of tithing, regularised in the Law of Moses, was already an accepted principle of worship (see 14:20).

QUESTION: What ought to be man's response to God's gracious revelation (see Rom. 12:1,2)?

Questions for further study and discussion on Genesis chapters 23-28

1. In what sense did Abraham rejoice to see the day of Christ (John 8:56)?

2. What part should Christian parents play in planning the marriages of their children? What criteria should determine the choice of a partner?

3. How can we reconcile the demands of courtesy and the principle that God's business requires haste (cf. 1 Sam. 21:8)?

4. What do we learn from the family life of Isaac and Rebekah? What other biblical families are a warning or an example to us?

5. 'Fear of man' proved to be his undoing. Consider the power which fear has over us. What is the antidote?

6. Why do you think 'peacemakers . . . shall be called sons of God' (Matt. 5:9)?

7. What are the effects of trying to do God's work in man's way?

8. Can any place really be called Bethel, 'the house of God' (see 1 Kings 8:27; Psa. 23:6;27:4)?

29 A hard school

Although twenty hard years (31:41) awaited Jacob in Haran there *was* an auspicious beginning. God had promised to guide him, and the principal purpose of his visit, to find a suitable wife (28:2), appeared almost immediately to be realised (4-10). Small wonder that Jacob, in a typically Oriental display of outward emotion, wept (11).

Jacob himself started well, emerging as the champion of Laban's daughter. It was customary to water the flocks when all were assembled, to avoid the chore of re-opening a well which was usually sealed by a stone needing two or three men to move it (2,3) – Jacob was evidently no stripling. His earlier stratagem (7) seems designed to get rid of the shepherds so that he could be alone with Rachel.

Laban, delighted with Jacob's arrival, may possibly have formally adopted his nephew (14). Jacob's mission clearly had a similar intention to the visit of Abraham's servant a full generation before (ch.24). Possibly the cunning Laban already entertained the idea of exploiting this situation, especially as Jacob's love for Rachel appears immediate and as deep as it was to prove lasting (20). The man, however, who had deceived his father and out-smarted his brother now found himself on the receiving end.

Laban's excuse (26) probably did reflect contemporary custom; it is widely attested in the ancient world (as is also the practice noted in vs.24,29). But in fact it underlines Laban's deceit. Why had he not enlightened Jacob when the request for Rachel was first made (18)? The problem of Jacob's failure to recognise Leah may be explained by two factors. First, it was traditional for the veiled bride to be brought to the bridegroom by night. Secondly, this was on the first night of a week-long feast (hence the reference in v.27; see also Judg. 14:12) when Jacob was probably intoxicated – Laban would make sure he was in no condition to thwart his plan. In the end, Laban gained a virtual slave-labourer for fourteen years since Jacob, unlike his father, was in no position to offer the customary marriage present to the parents of the prospective bride. Enmeshed in this sorry web of intrigue was Leah, initially Laban's accomplice, and wanting desperately to be loved (32,34), but always coming a poor second to Rachel. At least she was grateful to God for his mercies (32,35).

THOUGHT: 'The story reveals that God, not Laban, had the last word'. (Kidner)

Jacob's homecoming

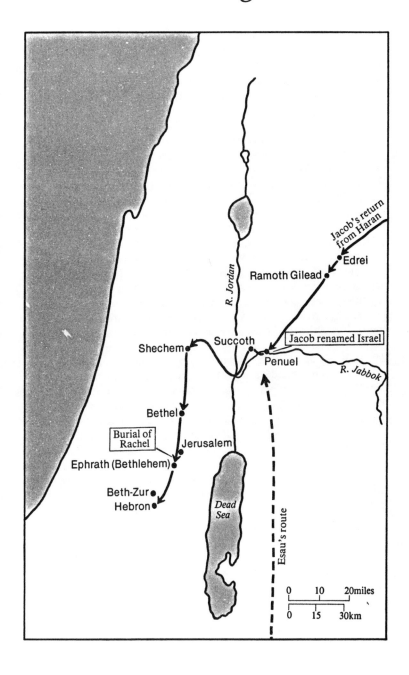

Jacob's return from Haran

Edrei

Ramoth Gilead

R. Jordan

Shechem

Succoth

Jacob renamed Israel

Penuel

R. Jabbok

Bethel

Burial of Rachel

Jerusalem

Ephrath (Bethlehem)

Beth-Zur

Hebron

Dead Sea

Esau's route

0   10   20miles

0   15   30km

30 Tension and intrigue

Against a background of envy, anger, petulance and reproach God continued to work out his purpose. This was in spite of the participants themselves, who frequently paid lip service to him (e.g. 6,18,20,23,24), but continued to act and react in a manner characterised by the flesh rather than the spirit. This attitude is clearly seen in the bargaining over mandrakes (14-18), the fruit and roots of which were believed to have aphrodisiac properties. Nonetheless the seeds of the future nation of Israel were sown here, and in a strange, almost prophetic, way the names given to the sons connect with the subsequent history of their tribes. The expression 'bear upon my knees' (3) indicates that the child born was reckoned publicly, and acknowledged personally, as legally adopted, in accordance with the custom prevailing (compare 16:2;50:23).

The birth of Joseph (25) seems to have jolted Jacob into an awareness of his basic problem, which was that he had no legal right to leave Laban, let alone leave in any degree of prosperity. This led to six years of intrigue between the two men (see 31:41), with Jacob ultimately outsmarting Laban. Lest we feel sorry for the latter, v.30 indicates the prosperity he owed to his nephew. But this is a sorry chapter, with the ring of hypocrisy in Laban's apparently frank assurance 'name your wages, and I will give it' (28), and Jacob's reference to 'my honesty' (33). Laban's ready acceptance of Jacob's suggestion (34), and his immediate counter-measures (35,36), suggest that he saw through Jacob's scheme from the start, but believed that he could outmanoeuvre him. Jacob's measures involved careful selection of stock (41,42), an established principle of husbandry, as well as the ancient notion that a startling vision had a corresponding influence upon the embryo. Whatever Jacob may have believed, the blessing of God was undoubtedly the principal factor (31:5,9).

Note: Verse 21. Almost certainly other daughters were born, but Dinah is mentioned in anticipation of ch.34.

THOUGHT: 'The prayer enshrined in the name [Joseph] is a good example of faith pressing on for more than God has given.' (Kidner)

31 Crisis!

Verse 8 indicates that the agreement of ch.30 was changed several times (compare 31:41), with Jacob, through God's intervention, always coming off best. He was wise enough, however, to appreciate the limits to Laban's endurance. Increasing tension mounted between the two men (2), between Jacob and Laban's sons (1), and between Laban and his daughters, alienated by their father's avarice and trickery (14-16). They were thus ready to join Jacob in a venture for freedom, and Jacob was prepared for the guidance to return home (3,13). In the twenty years at Haran he had gained a family and had proved the reality of God's presence (5) and protection (7). There was a debit side, though. To spend such a long time in continual conflict with an unscrupulous Laban did not help in the development of high moral standards. Overall, however, God's hand was certainly in this episode; Esau's hostility had been given time to lessen, and Jacob's increasing faith enabled him to face up to a probable confrontation with his brother.

If 'Euphrates' is correct (21, the Hebrew merely mentions 'the river'), then Laban covered about 300 miles in eight days, indicating his anger and evil intentions, as do also his words and the necessity of direct divine restraint (29). His mock-indignation (26), overlaid with hypocrisy (27) and sarcasm (30), hardly suits his character. Jacob, for all his faults, had more right on his side, and eventually even he was goaded into bitter protest (36-42). Archaeological evidence from Nuzi reveals the importance of the household gods (19,30-35). Whoever possessed them (usually the main heir) had a distinct advantage in matters of inheritance. An important theme in this chapter concerns the help Jacob received from God contrasted with the disaster which nearly overtook Rachel by her theft of the household gods.

So a partnership which was always uneasy came to an end (43-55). Laban, like Abimelech (20:3;26:28), was prevented from pressing a material advantage by a restraining, divine power. Whilst the 'Mizpah' benediction (49) is frequently used to invoke the Lord's watchful care over us and our distant loved ones, its original context was a mutually-suspicious non-aggression pact. The pile of stones marked the boundary and was a visual reminder of vows undertaken, but the real witness was God himself.

OBSERVATION: Note how Jacob's faith increases at points of crisis, well illustrated in his surprisingly fearless testimony (42). Is this an invariable experience?

32 Encounter with God

This was the great crisis of Jacob's life, through which he came to know God in a new, deeply personal way. Fear of his wronged brother had never left him – a vivid reminder that the deceiver is always exposed to hatred and revenge (see Gal. 6:7). But Jacob displayed courage in taking the initiative himself to heal the rift (3), doubtless encouraged by the awareness of divine protection (1,2). There was no attempt to sneak back to Bethel undetected. The fact that Jacob crossed the Jabbok, which flows westward through Gilead into the Jordan, shows that he was heading directly for Esau's territory (22), with the clear intention of looking first for reconciliation with his brother (compare Christ's words, Matt. 5:24).

Jacob's deep-seated fear emerges with equal clarity, revealed by: (a) his grovelling language (4,5,18-20); (b) his reaction to Esau's prompt and apparently aggressive response (6-8). Esau's thirst for vengeance had probably long since disappeared, but he could not resist demonstrating his capacity for action; (c) his continued scheming to minimise, by sensible precautions, the effect of any attack (7,8); (d) in his ostentatious present to placate Esau (13-21), doubtless hoping that these evidences of his generosity would have a cumulative effect. But supremely (e) in his prayer, in which despair and faith mingle (9-12). He pleads God's promises, acknowledges God's gracious faithfulness and constancy, and confesses frankly both his utter unworthiness and continuing fears.

In this supreme crisis there arose the necessity of being completely alone with God (24). The agonising uncertainty about Esau's reaction, leaving a terrifying 'perhaps' (20), left him with no peace, and brought this usually self-sufficient schemer to the end of his tether, 'left alone' in more ways than one, bereft of courage and confidence, in a situation far beyond the capacity of his considerable resources. At this point he met God (24-30) and, characteristically, he struggled where others would have submitted. Only gradually does his awareness of the identity of his nocturnal Adversary grow upon him, and his desire to know God's name (27) was probably that he might retain control rather than be controlled. But ultimately, in clinging to God in complete weakness and desperate faith, he discovered the way of victory. From this point on there was more than a new name (28); there was a new character with a new, more attractive dimension.

QUESTION: Could Jacob have improved on his course of action?

33 Reconciliation, not revenge

S. R. Driver's comment on the encounter between God and Jacob at Peniel (32:30) is undoubtedly true, 'God is his real antagonist, not Esau; it is God whom his sins have offended'. It remained true that Jacob had also offended Esau, whom he had still to meet, and as we have noted, the spectre of his brother's vengeance had long haunted him.

However, because of his new-found faith in God, Jacob approached the confrontation with Esau without cowardice, although with apparent trepidation. Taking precautions to safeguard Rachel and Joseph (1,2) he first exposed himself to possible danger (3), a gesture of openness which may have finally won over Esau, although the latter appears naturally warm-hearted, with an interested concern for Jacob's family (5).

Jacob's gift was probably more than the first generous, unselfish action of his life, for Esau's acceptance of it would be a tacit recognition of the fact that old scores were now settled (11). Possibly, too, it helped to relieve Jacob's troubled conscience, which was rendered more sensitive by Esau's full and unconditional forgiveness. Obviously, Esau did not need Jacob's gift, for God had evidently prospered him. Jacob's reference to 'seeing the face of God' (10) draws attention to the fact that God is as clearly revealed in his overruling of events as in the personal encounter with him (32:30).

Jacob continued to be somewhat mistrustful, and was obviously relieved when both Esau and his men departed (12-16). There is no evidence that he ever visited Esau at Seir (14). Their only other recorded meeting was at Isaac's funeral (35:29). Instead, he stayed for a considerable but unspecified time at Succoth (17), just westwards of Peniel, before recrossing the Jordan and settling at Shechem (18,19). Here he built what was presumably his first altar, declaring his faith openly by the use of his new name, Israel (20, compare 32:28). So his promise a generation before was honoured (28:20-22), as were all God's promises to him (28:13-15).

Note: Verse 3, 'bowing . . . seven times', an extreme form of homage normally reserved for kings or the highest dignitaries.

THOUGHT: God is as clearly revealed in his overruling of events as in the personal encounter with him.

34 Cruel wrath (49:7)

Shechem, mentioned frequently in contemporary records, is shown by archaeology to have been an important city dominating the valley between Mts. Ebal and Gerizim. In a land largely inhabited by Semitic peoples these Hivites (2) were distinguished by their uncircumcised state. Centuries later the Shechemites were still being called 'the men of Hamor the father of Shechem' (Judg. 9:28) in another ugly incident illustrating the tension between Israel and the local inhabitants. This chapter reminds us of the fallibility of the early patriarchs, and highlights the integrity of the biblical record, which makes no attempt to whitewash them.

Dinah, at the time of her rape (2), and abduction (26), cannot have been more than about fourteen, since Joseph, about one year her junior (30:21-24), was only seventeen when the events of ch.37 took place (37:2). Whilst Jacob took no immediate action (5), possibly attracted by the prospect of local security, riches and prestige (9-12), his sons planned revenge, masquerading under the guise of friendliness which reached the ultimate in hypocrisy by its abuse of the sacred covenantal sign of circumcision (13-17). The after-effects of this would incapacitate the men of Shechem, whose deceitful motivation is also exposed (23). Murder and pillage resulted, far beyond even the bounds of revenge accepted in a primitive society (25-29). At the other end of the scale of reactions was Jacob's apparent lack of concern over these grave moral issues. His interest appears purely self-centred at this stage (30), although 49:5-7 shows his later capacity for a more objective judgement.

Notes: Verse 7, 'folly in Israel'. Already there was the awareness of a separated community. 'Folly' refers to any act which contravened accepted standards and so shocked moral sense (compare Josh. 7:15; Judg. 20:6; 2 Sam. 13:12). Verse 30: 'if' marks an important consideration, which facilitated Israel's settlement and ultimate possession of the land. Local rivalries *always* precluded that effective co-operation which could easily have driven out a numerically inferior Israel (compare Deut. 7:7,17-23).

TO THINK OVER: Was life at this time essentially different from our modern society? Can God's grace still operate in an apparently godless setting (see 1 Cor. 6:9-11)?

Questions for further study and discussion on Genesis chapters 29-34

1. Why did God allow Jacob to develop in such a dubious environment?

2. How far does Laban illustrate the truth that people are most sensitive and self-righteous when hurt in matters where they themselves are most guilty? What does that suggest about our own failures?

3. Is there anyone who need not say 'I am not worthy . . .' (32:10)?

4. What can we learn about our own relationship with God from Jacob's wrestling match at the Jabbok?

5. How far is fear, or doubt, compatible with faith?

6. What is the relationship between being reconciled to God and getting right with our fellow men?

7. What can we learn from ch.34 about the principles which ought to govern relationships between diverse groups living in close proximity?

35 A vow fulfilled

1. The return to Bethel (1-8). God's pointed intervention (1) seems to have shaken Jacob out of his spiritual apathy. Why had he not returned to Bethel earlier to honour his promises (28:20-22), especially after the broad hint of 31:13? Was Shechem marginally farther away from Esau, or were its rich pastures more attractive than Bethel, which at 2890 feet, was over a thousand feet higher (note v.1, 'go up')? From God's point of view, all that occurred between Jacob's departure from Laban and his arrival at Bethel appears incidental (9). Now, at last, Jacob was impelled to share his faith (3), calling his family to a personal sanctification ('purify yourselves', compare Exod. 19:10,14,15) and consecration (2). In fact, acknowledgment of the foreign gods which originated in Mesopotamia was *not* eliminated at this time (compare Josh. 24:14,15). 'Rings' (4) were worn as charms as well as ornaments. Total loyalty to God, then as now, involves the rejection of *all* lesser trusts. A later generation, aware from bitter experience of the perils of idolatry, dealt more drastically with 'foreign gods' than Jacob did (see Deut. 12:3; 2 Kings 23:4-14). One sad note comes in, the death of Deborah, Rebekah's nurse, who must have been extremely old (see 24:59). How she became attached to Jacob's household is not recorded.

2. The renewal of blessing (9-15). When man is repentant and obedient a long-suffering God always matches his response with divine grace (compare Ps. 103:8-14). Now the covenantal promises were reaffirmed personally to Jacob (11,12). Verse 10 (compare 32:28) is not a variant account of Jacob's new name but rather an indication that now he was worthy of it. But, even in a time of spiritual exaltation, the man of God is not immune from sorrow, highlighted here by the death of Jacob's beloved Rachel (19). Human relationships are interrupted by death (compare Ps. 146:3-7), but our fellowship with God never is (see Pss. 16:10,11; 73:23-26; 102:27).

Note: Verse 19: 'Ephrath' appears to be identified with Bethlehem in Ruth 4:11 and Mic. 5:2, whereas 1 Sam. 10:2 and Jer. 31:15 set it at Ramah, *north* of Jerusalem, in the territory of Benjamin. Verse 19 (compare 48:7) simply notes that Rachel died 'on the way to Ephrath'. The traditional site is located one mile north of Bethlehem.

FOR THOUGHT: One rash act cost Reuben his birthright (22, see 1 Chron. 5:1, compare Esau in 25:29-34).

36 Edomite history

The importance of Edom, and the continuing divine concern for it, are demonstrated by this chapter. The parting of the ways between Esau and Jacob (6,7), reminiscent of that between Abraham and Lot (13:5-12), must have occurred at an earlier date, since Esau was well settled in Edom when Jacob returned from Paddan-aram (32:3;33:14,16). Archaeology shows that the territory of Edom was settled during the period 2300–2000 BC followed by a break in occupation, possibly caused by the invasion of Chedorlaomer and his allies (14:1-12). Esau's marriage to Oholibamah attests an alliance with the surviving Horite remnant (2,20-25, the Hivites and Horites are to be equated); she was the daughter of a local chieftain. Esau's family (15-19,40-43) thereafter ruled in accordance with the local pattern until the Edomites adopted a monarchic form of government (31-39), long before the anointing of the first Israelite king.

Despite the blood-tie between the two nations relationships were never warm, in spite of the exhortation of Deut. 23:7. Edom refused to allow Israel to pass through its territory after the Exodus (Num. 20:14-21), necessitating a lengthy detour (Num. 21:4). Both Saul (1 Sam. 14:47) and David (2 Sam. 8:13,14) campaigned against the Edomites. At one point in David's reign an attempt seems to have been made to eradicate Edom (1 Kings 11:15-17). At a later date Edom was allied with Ammon and Moab against Judah (2 Chron. 20), and a glance at a concordance will show many other instances of mutual hostility. From Judah's point of view, the culminating point was Edom's treachery in harrying her when defenceless after the Babylonian overthrow of Jerusalem in 587 BC. Most of the exilic and post-exilic writers express bitter indignation over this (e.g. Ps. 137:7; Lam. 4:21,22; Ezek. 35:1-15: Obad. 5-16; Mal. 1:4).

Note: Verse 12. The origin of the Amalekites, who figured prominently in Israel's history from the Exodus to the early monarchy, is noted here. Verse 37, 'the Euphrates', should probably be translated literally, 'the river', referring to a local river rather than the Euphrates itself, which was, of course, not in the area of Edom.

37 Spotlight on Joseph

Genesis 36, dealing with Edom, comes at a natural break in the narrative. Isaac is dead (35:29), Jacob still continues, but the focus is already on Joseph. Had Jacob profited from his own unfortunate family background he would have realised the pernicious effects of favouritism. Untold misery had resulted from Isaac's partiality for Esau, and Rebekah's compensating championing of Jacob. In spite of this, however, Jacob's preference for Joseph was obvious, and the latter's character, as well as the family unity, suffered. Stephen, in Acts 7, argues powerfully that, as ancient Israel had rejected her deliverers, including Joseph, so the Jews had rejected Christ. But there is a difference. Jesus was completely innocent whilst Joseph, somewhat spoilt and precocious, did provide fuel for his brothers' hatred. He may have been justified in tale-telling (2), since it is not always easy to draw the line between loyalty to one's fellows and responsibility towards one's superiors. But whilst his first dream may have been told innocently, his brothers' sharp reaction (8) ought to have cautioned him to keep the second one to himself (9-11). Instead he incurred their increasing hostility and the rebuke of his father. Later on, he was surely unwise in wearing his long-sleeved garment – the symbol of special favour (see 2 Sam. 13:18,19) – when sent to enquire after his brothers at Shechem (fifty miles from Hebron; Dothan was a further fifteen miles). This must have infuriated them, especially as the traditional chore of the youngest son was 'keeping the sheep' (compare 1 Sam. 16:11), for which a more serviceable short-length, sleeveless garment would be worn.

Reuben's concern to save Joseph (21-24) was not completely disinterested, for as the oldest son he faced the responsibility of breaking any bad news to his father, and circumstances were to show just how hard this would be (31-35). Sin, when unconfessed, always leads to further sin. It needs a cover-up story and Joseph's brothers had henceforth to live with their lie, constantly fearful that in an unguarded moment the truth might slip out. Even they must have suffered when they witnessed the agony which their cruel deceit had inflicted on their father (34,35). However, at that moment when rough, unbrotherly hands seized Joseph (23) God began the preparation, prolonged and painful, of his chosen servant.

QUESTION: Can God use apparent misfortunes to fulfil such a function in our lives?

38 Judah and Tamar

This chapter, seemingly an unsavoury intrusion, is important for its concentration on Judah, whose tribe was eventually to become dominant, ultimately providing the Messiah. Already we have been shown Judah's heartless, grasping nature (37:26) and the same tendency is revealed here. Away from the restraining influence of home he 'went down' (1), physically from the highlands of Hebron, but morally and spiritually by his association with the Canaanites (2). Judah later became the acknowledged leader among his brothers and shows a remarkable transformation of character, but at this time any example is towards evil and the degradation which resulted is obvious. His first-born, Er, was too evil to be left alive (7). The second, Onan, was too selfish, consistently (v.9 'when' should be translated 'whenever') attempting to cheat Tamar of her legal right to an heir, probably because he himself would forfeit the right of the first-born if successful. This custom of levirate marriage, defined in Deut. 25:5-10, was widely practised in the ancient world. Designed to prevent the extinction of a family line and name it was, in fact, often inconvenient, as the story of Ruth demonstrates. Tamar's deception involved masquerading as a cult-prostitute (the meaning of 'harlot', v.15). Existing to encourage the nature gods to promote fertility on a wider scale, this group, including both sexes, was amongst the most evil features of the sensual Canaanite religion. Sheep-shearing (13) was traditionally a time for uninhibited licentiousness. But Tamar, with both Onan and Judah determined to prevent legal rights, demonstrates considerable courage, facing the possible penalty of v.24, whereas Judah sees the death penalty as a cowardly way out of his predicament, hence his confession (26).

The sheer grace of God also appears from a consideration of this chapter. How incredible it is that Tamar the Canaanite and Perez, the child of this degraded union, share in the genealogy of Christ (Matt. 1:3)! But Rahab the harlot, Ruth the Moabitess and Manasseh and Amon (rendered Amos in some versions), the two worst kings of Judah, are there also. For those from humble or blighted backgrounds (see 1 Cor. 6:9-11) there is no reason for a debilitating inferiority complex – the grace of God is sufficient to transform the ugliest situation. Indeed, all of us were 'no hopers' in his sight (Eph. 2:12)!

Note: Verse 18. The 'signet' would be a cylindrical seal, equivalent to a personal signature.

39 Joseph's further humiliation

Potiphar (1) is probably an abbreviated Hebrew form of Potiphera, meaning 'he whom P'Ra (the sun god) has given'. His main function as 'captain of the guard' was the oversight of the prison system; possibly also he may have been responsible for Pharaoh's bodyguard. It is likely that this particular Pharaoh was one of the early members of the Hyksos dynasty (1720–1570 BC) who, being Semitic, showed considerable partiality to other Semitic groups, an important point to remember when considering the treatment later given to Jacob's family.

On the surface this is a chapter of misfortune, during which Joseph, already rejected by his brothers and sold into slavery, was plagued by alternating limited success and seeming disaster. Falsely accused (the fact that Potiphar did not inflict the usual death-penalty may suggest his doubts concerning the accuracy of the charge), and his reputation ruined, it could have seemed that disaster was dogging Joseph's steps. The central fact in this chapter, however, is 'the Lord was with Joseph' (2-6,21-23) and this kept him *silent* in the face of false accusation; *serene* in his inner spirit; and *steadfast* in the face of multiplied misfortune. Without doubt his character was moulded by this experience. Evidently God became real and personal to him at this time, perhaps just because of the shock of this sudden reversal of his fortunes. In comparison with ch.37 Joseph appears as a changed character; faithful in limited areas (2,22), he proved himself worthy of a greater trust. There was an obvious quality about his witness (3,23). So Joseph becomes a timeless witness to the difference which results when the Lord is with a person, irrespective of outward condition. There is no pathway of adversity so narrow that it separates us from the Lord; no night so dark that the Light of the world is extinguished; no situation which he is unable to use for the enrichment of our character and the ultimate outworking of his will.

Note: Verse 1: 'Ishmaelites', used alternately with Midianites (compare 37:25,28; Judg. 8:24). *Midianites* indicates their nationality; *Ishmaelites* refers to their function as nomadic, gipsy-type traders. Verse 6: the Egyptians, like the Hebrews, had rigid laws concerning food. Verse 14: there is an obvious slight in the use of the term 'Hebrew'.

THOUGHT: There is no pathway of adversity so narrow that it separates us from the Lord; no night so dark that the Light of the world is extinguished.

Questions for further study and discussion on Genesis chapters 35–39

1. In religious reformation are external and inward factors always involved?

2. In what circumstances should a Christian report obvious wrong doing to his superior? What are the limits to loyalty to one's fellow-workers?

3. Does God still use the biblical method of revelation through dreams? Is there instead, or also, a more direct and personal way? See John 16:13.

4. How, in the light of Gen. 38 and the later significance of Judah, should we behave towards those who are guilty of moral failure?

5. Joseph's brothers were prepared to sell him for twenty shekels. In what ways can we be guilty of placing too low a value on human life?

6. Consider Rom. 8:28 in relationship to Joseph and your own experience.

40 'Endurance produces character'

Psalm 105:16-19 outlines the sufferings endured by Joseph, and observes that 'the word of the Lord tested him'. It is comparatively easy to bear a heavy burden for a limited period, but when it has to be long endured, and disappointments follow in swift succession, then true character has the opportunity to reveal itself. Although Joseph was unaware of it, God, through the hard school of painful experience, was preparing him for his vital future role of deliverer.

Already certain commendable traits of character are observable: (a) Joseph was obviously sympathetic, alert to the moods and needs of his fellow prisoners (6,7). The rank injustice he had suffered had in no way soured him. (b) His bearing, therefore, invited confidence. Clearly he was approachable. Officially, he was merely a convicted Hebrew slave, the servant of higher-ranking prisoners, but *they* obviously trusted him. (c) He remained sure of the presence and help of God (8). Prison walls and tight security are no barrier to fellowship with an ever-present, all-powerful God, as Paul and Silas (Acts 16:25;23:11) and countless others up to and including our own generation (can you think of examples?) have discovered. (d) His willingness to attempt interpretations of the two dreams indicates his faith that his own dreams would be fulfilled (37:5-10). There is no hint of disenchantment. Hope might be long deferred, but the outcome was sure. The Egyptians, even more than the Hebrews, set great store on the significance of dreams. A great deal of literature on the subject had been produced, but probably this was unavailable to these prisoners; hence their concern. (e) Ingratitude and forgetfulness can hurt deeply and Joseph suffered these for two further years (41:1). In fact, higher hands were in control. God had his own perfect time for deliverance coincidental with Joseph's perfect opportunity.

Notes: Verse 15, 'I was indeed stolen'. Note how, in this context, Joseph generalises, softening the embarrassing and humiliating fact that his brothers had sold him. In another context he has no hesitation in stating the blunt truth (45:5;50:20). Verse 20, 'lift up your head' (13). The verb indicates a restoration to favour; compare Jehoiachin's elevation from his Babylonian prison (2 Kings 25:27, KJV), and the use of a *different* verb of God's favour in Ps. 3:3;27:6. What appears as a gruesome pun in v.19 would be safeguarded by Joseph's attitude and tone of voice.

THOUGHT: Prison walls and tight security are no barrier to fellowship with an ever-present, all-powerful God.

41 'Favour and wisdom' (Acts 7:10)

The gods were believed to reveal the future through dreams. Dreams before special occasions were particularly significant; hence the disquiet of the butler and baker before Pharaoh's birthday – the traditional occasion for the release or sentencing of prisoners. The dreams of kings acquired an even greater importance when repeated in detail as here (1-7). In Egypt and Mesopotamia (e.g. Dan. 2;4) dreams were interpreted through professional 'wise men', but in Israel the interpretation was usually self-evident (e.g. 37:5-10). Whilst God continued to use dreams as a means of revelation (e.g. Matt. 1:20;2:12,13), the method became suspect in Israel because of its misuse by false prophets (Jer. 23:25-28).

Joseph's poise and perception are inexplicable apart from the fact that he was in touch with God, humble, consciously dependent, and giving him *all* the glory (16). His authority was such that no one questioned the interpretation which he offered. Both of Pharaoh's dreams had an ominous significance, but Joseph was enabled to see how the period of plenty could be utilised to cover the future emergency (28-36). So he came into Pharaoh's presence as a prisoner, and went out prime-minister. This 'fairy-story' element should not cause the narrative to be dismissed as legendary. The details accord perfectly with Egyptian customs, and truth is invariably stranger than fiction because fiction is bound to appear credible. Moreover, it must not be overlooked that thirteen years of repeated rejection, suffering, humiliation and disappointment preceded this moment (46, see 37:2). Joseph's sterling qualities had been forged in a fiery furnace. Pharaoh was not the first to recognise Joseph's qualities and put complete trust in him (compare 39:3,4,21-23). The real source of these was not unique to Joseph, however; it is the Spirit of God (38), who throughout Scripture is the source of wisdom and insight (Exod. 31:3; Num. 27:18; Ezek. 36:27; Eph. 1:17).

Notes: Verse 45. Joseph's new, elevated position was marked by a new name of uncertain meaning. 'On', later called Heliopolis, seven miles north-east of Cairo, was the centre of worship of the sun-god, whose name appears in the final syllable of Potiphe*ra*.

THOUGHT: Prosperity can easily lead to forgetfulness, but Joseph continued to acknowledge God's goodness (50-52). And the sons born in Egypt by his Egyptian wife were given Hebrew names. He knew the destiny of his people (see 50:24,25).

42 The brothers' trial, I

Since Egypt and Canaan were affected by different climatic and natural factors (e.g. the vital importance of the Nile in Egypt), a famine which included both was unusual. Jacob possibly suspected his sons' involvement in Joseph's disappearance. He appears unwilling to entrust Benjamin to them (4), and he comments on their reluctance to go to Egypt (1, see also v.36).

A high official like Joseph would not normally personally interview applicants for relief. Perhaps, anticipating his brothers' eventual arrival, he had made arrangements to identify them. Would he realise, in their first encounter, the fulfilment of his dream (6, see 37:5-8)? The difference in his appearance from youth to middle-age, his Egyptian clothing, and the complete improbability of finding him in such an eminent position would preclude their recognition of him. Joseph has been accused of harshness, but surely he required adequate proof of a fundamental change in his brothers, and he could ensure this only by subjecting them to pressure. It must have been hard to restrain his natural impulse for an early reunion with Jacob and Benjamin, especially when he detected signs of change in his brothers. No longer was he 'this dreamer' (37:19), but 'our brother' (21), 'the lad' (22) and, though they thought him dead, they still included him in the family circle (13). Note also their acute sense of sin, and their confession that a just judgement had overtaken them (22). But more than this was required. One can appreciate the dreadful sense of foreboding felt first by the brothers (28) and then by Jacob (35). Joseph could easily construe the situation as one of theft. So Simeon, never the favourite of Jacob (34:25,30; 49:5-7), was abandoned, but there is an element of selfishness in Jacob's reaction (36,38). Reuben again appears weak and unstable (49:4). Earlier, his attempt to save Joseph had been foiled (37:21-29), and he had indulged in useless recriminations (42:22). There was also a definite moral weakness (35:22). Here, his apparently sacrificial offer (37) was rash and unbalanced (compare Judah's in 43:9).

Notes: Verse 15, 'by the life of Pharaoh'. Since Pharaoh was regarded as divine, this was clearly a powerful oath. Verses 30,33 *'the'* man'. In view of the attitude to Pharaoh, this indicates the leading man in Egypt. Verse 38, 'Sheol'. The shadowy abode of all the departed, without distinction, where all but the barest existence ceased (see Job 3:13-19).

THOUGHT: God also tests character thoroughly, and with transforming results (Rom. 5:3,4).

43 The brothers' trial, II

Whilst the focus of attention is naturally upon Joseph, the main point of these chapters is to show how the brothers were tested by prolonged stress, as Joseph himself had been. In this crisis it was Judah who emerged as the leader – a significant point in the light of the later dominance of his tribe. Indications of a developing character are shown in the firm, matter-of-fact way in which he dealt with his aged, short-tempered and indecisive father (3-5,10), but especially in his willingness to accept *personal* responsibility for Benjamin (9), in contrast to Reuben's 'guarantee' involving the lives of others (42:37). Jacob himself remains self-centred (6), with no apparent concern for the imprisoned Simeon. Whilst it was virtually obligatory to approach a person of rank with a gift (see 1 Sam. 16:20;17:18), there is also a suggestion of his old capacity for shrewd management of a difficult situation. A generous gift had worked wonders with Esau (32:13-21); perhaps it would do the same with this 'Egyptian' official (11). The use of the covenantal name 'God Almighty' (14; see 17:1), however, may well have been a 'desperate plea of faith' concerning his family's promised destiny.

The second encounter of the brothers with Joseph was a traumatic experience for them. They regarded the banquet in their honour as a trap (16-19), and took exaggerated care in protesting their innocence (20-22). Their apprehension was obvious (23), their attitude was servile (26,28), and their amazement at Joseph's apparently supernatural knowledge (33) was unbounded. However, the tension gradually relaxed (34), which made the dramatic reversal of fortune in ch.44 the more frightening. Joseph's strength of character in carrying through this elaborate test is noteworthy. He had a purpose, and the temporary unpleasantness it caused his whole family was therefore worthwhile.

It is noteworthy that a new dimension of love is introduced here. Whilst the bond between husband and wife (Jacob and Rachel), and father and son (Abraham and Isaac), had been well illustrated, brotherly love had been conspicuously absent (e.g. Cain and Abel, Ishmael and Isaac, Jacob and Esau). Joseph's deep love for Benjamin reveals a refreshingly welcome picture of a tender brotherly affection.

Note: Verse 23: Simeon's confinement was probably well under two years (see 45:6).

44 The final test

All must have seemed well as the brothers pursued their homeward journey. Simeon had been released and Benjamin was still safe. The arrival of Joseph's steward plunged them back into a nightmarish experience. Theft would be the more reprehensible in view of: (a) Joseph's generous hospitality; (b) the overweight grain sacks (1), and (c) the personal and sacred character of the stolen article (4,5). Divination by water was widely practised at this time, although the suggestion that Joseph performed this (15) may have been part of a fabrication designed to convince the brothers that uncanny, irresistible powers were working against them. Years before they had disposed of Joseph for a paltry sum. Now they had an opportunity for abandoning another brother for a much greater gain – their own freedom. *Twice* they rejected this chance to save their own skins (10,17). They were not tempted to desert Benjamin, nor was there any recrimination against him, although they must have assumed his guilt. Instead, their immediate reaction was to return to Egypt and share Benjamin's slavery (13,16). 'God has found out the guilt of your servants' (16) was more than an admission of collective guilt; it certainly had overtones of their guilty consciences concerning their treatment of Joseph. Ancient Israel was beginning to take shape in this sense of family solidarity to the point of mutually shared suffering. In the third confrontation with Joseph, which forms a dramatic climax, Reuben, the first-born, is silent. It is Judah, already the accepted leader (14) and spokesman (16), who petitions the apparently obdurate Joseph. To return without Benjamin would be to write Jacob's death sentence (30,31). Judah reveals: (a) a sympathy with Jacob conspicuously missing when he was the ringleader in disposing of Joseph (31,34; compare 37:26,27); (b) an appreciation of the peculiarly intimate relationship between Jacob and Benjamin (30,31) without any of the resentment formerly shown to Joseph (37:4,8,11); (c) an acceptance, to the point of self-sacrifice, of the responsibility he had assumed for Benjamin's safety (32,33). In this there is a hint of the Saviour, of the tribe of Judah, who gave himself vicariously for a condemned world.

The sheer literary brilliance of the narrative, especially the gripping suspense when Joseph is testing his brothers, should not be overlooked.

QUESTION: To what extent are we required to show 'family solidarity' in sharing the misfortunes of our fellow-Christians?

45 Climax

The crux of the whole ordeal to which Joseph had subjected his brothers concerned their character – *had* they changed radically, or *would* they abandon Benjamin? Judah's utterly selfless appeal (44:18-34), showing both brotherly and filial love, meant that Joseph, faced with such evidence of a genuine repentance, could drop further deception and reveal himself. However, the ordeal of the brothers was not yet over (3); indeed it was suddenly magnified alarmingly. They were completely within the power of the one they had once hated and rejected. Their fear and guilty conscience were obvious (5). But Joseph was aware of a divine overruling. Not that he minimised his brothers' guilt; from the human angle they had sold him (4,5). However, there was a wiser, stronger hand than theirs – 'God sent me before you to preserve life' (5,7; see Psa. 105:17). Both elements had their place, but only one was fundamental . . . 'it was not . . . you, *but God*' (8; see 50:20). Here, then, was a classic example of the truth, 'God works in *everything* for good' (Rom. 8:28). After long, painful years Joseph, like Abraham's servant, could both affirm 'God led me by the right way' *and* give glory to God (8;24:27,48).

Joseph's humanity emerges in the twice repeated 'make haste' (9,13), showing how much he yearned for reunion with his aged father (compare Paul's longing for human friendship in 2 Tim. 4:9,21). There is another delightfully human touch in v.24. Joseph, an excellent judge of character, knew that there could be arguments amongst the brothers (see 42:22); especially when they contemplated telling the whole story to Jacob, when their earlier cruel deceit about Joseph was bound to emerge. Jacob himself, having perhaps too readily presumed Joseph's death (37:33), now found it difficult to accept that he was alive (26) – possibly it seemed too good to be true. Yet how often the Lord does surprise us with his goodness! For Jacob, the well-laden wagons were (characteristically?) the necessary proof. When he said, 'I will go . . .' (28) it initiated a new era, ultimately painful and yet decisive. Isolated as foreigners during the long sojourn in Egypt, Jacob's clan would be free to develop into a nation.

Note: Verse 8: 'a father to Pharaoh', a common description of a ruler's trusted counsellor; compare Jehoash's attitude to Elisha (2 Kings 13:14).

THOUGHT: 'And we know that in all things God works together for the good of those who love him, who have been called according to his purpose' (Rom. 8:28, NIV)

Questions for further study and discussion on Genesis chapters 40-45

1. In the light of 41:33-36 what is the balance between sensible preparation (e.g. Prov. 6:6-11;30:25) and that faith which precludes anxious care (Matt. 6:25)?

2. How does your knowledge of God assist you in facing life's problems? What can we learn from the example of Joseph?

3. Can you account for the disunity and weaknesses within Jacob's family?

4. Was Joseph's isolation from the Egyptians (43:32) a mark of deference to his position, or did he, too, share the separation of being a Hebrew (Heb. 11:26)? What treatment should the Christian expect from the society in which he lives?

5. Is it possible to determine any of the factors which led to the brothers' change of attitude? Do they teach us any general lessons about human nature?

6. Work out the comparisons and contrasts between Joseph and the prodigal son (Luke 15:11-24).

7. Was Joseph justified in subjecting his brothers to this lengthy ordeal? What responsibility do Christian leaders have to assess the standing of others (especially perhaps new converts, applicants for baptism, church membership)? How should they go about it?

46 Israel in Egypt

Events at Beer-sheba showed that Jacob, although already *en route* to Egypt, needed the divine assurance. Beer-sheba, associated so closely with events in the lives of Abraham and Isaac, must have appeared a natural place for his act of thanksgiving and consecration (1). Note how God reminds him that the ground of his faith is in a past experience (3, 'the God of your father'). Isaac had proved God true, now Jacob is invited to prove God's promises for his future (3,4). Without the fundamental promise, 'I will go down with you' (4), it would have been a pointless journey (compare Matt. 28:18-20). The genealogical list (8-27) is important since it documents the relatively small group which was to develop, miraculously, into a nation (compare Deut. 10:22).

Judah is again found in the place of responsibility (28). The main interest, however, is in Joseph's deliberate policy (29-34). Even in the joy of reunion he did not lose sight of God's overall purposes. In spite of his important position at Pharaoh's court, he knew that Egypt was not to be Israel's permanent home. Hence his carefully-explained scheme to settle his family in the land of Goshen, usually identified with the *Wadi Tumilat*, an area of excellent pasture-land, east of the main areas of Egyptian settlement. John Skinner describes it as 'a weak spot in the natural defences of Egypt', so it was strategically situated from Joseph's point of view as the logical point of departure for the promised land. Similarly the brothers, by stressing that they were a nomadic people ('keepers of cattle', 34), would be kept separate and thus preserve their tribal identity. There is considerable evidence from Egyptian inscriptions showing that herdsmen were regarded as a socially inferior class. Some degree of integration was inevitable (see Exod. 1:12;3:22), but Joseph's motive for this policy of maximum isolation is made clear in 50:24,25.

Note: Verse 34. 'Goshen' is elsewhere called 'the land of Rameses' (47:11), and 'the fields of Zoan' (Ps. 78:12,43).

THOUGHT: Without the fundamental promise, 'I will go down with you' it would have been a pointless journey.

47 Ruthless – or realistic?

Jacob's characteristically pessimistic view of life again emerges. Almost everything recorded of him since Joseph's blood-stained coat was presented to him (37:35) has some reference to his death. His words in v.9 could display typically Oriental self-deprecation, but they could well be factual. Life almost always appears brief in retrospect, and Jacob's life was dominated generally by self-interest. When, in contrast, life is lived in conformity with God's standards and for his glory; when the maximum help is lovingly given to our fellows; when self-giving, not self-concern, is paramount, there can be few regrets. Joseph himself, who as a young man appeared full of self-interest, broke free and is a witness to these truths.

Joseph has, however, been accused of being a hard bargainer, gaining from the Egyptians their cash (14), cattle (17) and their very selves (19). Commentators have pointed out the dangers of a totalitarian state, especially when an autocrat, less humane and well intentioned than Joseph, assumes control. But the narrative itself appears warmly commendatory. The Egyptians themselves, by their ungrudging testimony (25), show no bitterness; to them liberty was a small price to pay for life. Joseph's wise stewardship was, in fact, remarkably considerate. True, the land, apart from the priestly possessions, became Pharaoh's, as in theory it had always been, since Pharaoh was regarded as the embodiment of the gods. The Egyptians became tenant farmers on exceptionally generous terms: a twenty per cent tax (24) was remarkably low, especially as: (a) the initial seed was provided (23); (b) the productivity of Egypt was proverbial, and (c) the current rate of taxation was greatly higher elsewhere, and remains so today, not merely in countries with oppressive systems of land-tenure but in almost all of the developed countries. Technically, however, freedom was lost, since personal freedom in ancient Egypt was linked with land ownership. Note that personal slavery was allowed under later Israelite law (e.g. Lev. 25:44–46).

Like Joseph, Jacob was convinced that his people's future was not in Mesopotamia, the land of their origin; or Egypt, the country which seemed to offer security and prosperity; but in Canaan, the land of promise (29-31). So he faced death openly and with faith. The vow with the hand under the thigh (29, see 24:2) was particularly binding.

QUESTION: In what circumstances if any, should religious groups have special state privileges (see v.22)?

48 Faith finally flowers

Faith was operative in both Jacob and Joseph. Joseph could have used his influential position to advance the career prospects of his sons in Egypt; instead, in bringing them to his father, he shows the kind of blessing he desired for them. Jacob foresaw the time when the promise to the patriarchs (3,4) would be fulfilled. Within this inheritance Joseph would have the double portion, the honour of the first-born (Deut. 21:17; 2 Kings 2:9). So Ephraim and Manasseh were now formally adopted as Jacob's sons and direct heirs (5), symbolised by their being placed by or between Jacob's knees (12; see 50:23). Many have seen in this ceremony an anticipation of the way in which Christian believers, brought near by Christ, are adopted into God's family.

There was also a prophetic element in Jacob's faith. He himself, as the younger son, had wrested the birthright from Esau. In contrast, he now quietly and deliberately gives the younger son the blessing of the first-born, in spite of Joseph's protests. Throughout Scripture the laying on of hands signifies the conveyance of rights and privileges, and the right hand is especially favoured. Historically Ephraim did become the strongest tribe, particularly in the earlier period of settlement, when Ephraim and Manasseh occupied about half the total area conquered. Hosea and others use Ephraim as a synonym for the entire Northern Kingdom (e.g. Hos. 5:3; Ps. 78:67). The 'mountain slope' (22) is literally 'Shecham', the scene of earlier settlement and slaughter (33:18-34:31). Midway between Ephraim and Manasseh, and roughly central in the whole land, it became the place of Joseph's burial and the rallying point of the tribes.

Jacob's faith reaches its highest point in his testimony and blessing (15,16). It stresses the fact of covenantal continuity, involving the past (Abraham and Isaac), the present (Jacob himself), and the future (Joseph's sons and their descendants). Jacob's experience was warmly personal and redemptive (16a) – he knew the evil from which he had been preserved. God, as his 'Redeemer-kinsman', the establisher and maintainer of family rights (e.g. Ruth 3:2-4), had championed his cause and preserved him. The word 'led' (15) is better translated 'shepherded', introducing a complementary metaphor, its first use in Scripture (see Ps. 23; Isa. 40:11; Jer. 31:10; Ezek. 34:12-16, 23). All this formed a rich heritage which Jacob was concerned to share.

THOUGHT: Men die ... God is always alive (21, see Ps. 146:3-7; Isa. 6:1).

49 The future foretold

The importance attached to the patriarchal blessing, a form of predictive prophecy, is further attested here. *Reuben* (3,4) was the epitome of unrealised potential, promising so much and accomplishing so little because of his instability – the word conveys the thought of recklessness. Similar in tone was the oracle concerning *Dan* (16-18), but, whereas Reuben's failure was moral weakness, Dan's was a treacherous nature. The tribe of Dan, weakened in the early generations of settlement (in Judg. 13:2;18:11 it is referred to as 'the family of the Danites'), is here depicted as realising full tribal status. *Simeon and Levi* were brothers in violence and viciousness (5-7) – an allusion to 34:25-31. This prophecy was fulfilled in strangely diverse ways: Simeon became absorbed into Judah; Levi vindicated itself by loyalty to the Lord (Exod. 32:25-29), and its dispersion was for responsible, priestly service (Num. 18:23). *Judah* (8-12) receives disproportionate treatment, and the range of prophecy includes a messianic element. It is the conquering, kingly tribe (8-10), and the imagery extends to the universal rule and absolute prosperity (10-12) of the prophetic 'Golden Age' (e.g. Isa. 9:6,7;11:1-9), fulfilled in Christ (see Rev. 5:5). *Zebulun and Issachar* (13-15) are spoken of in sarcastic terms. In close proximity to Phoenicia, both gained prosperity by partially surrendering their independence. *Gad* (19), a Transjordan tribe, suffered frequent border raids. *Asher and Naphtali* (20,21) are described in terms of contentment. The former settled in the highly productive strip north of Mt. Carmel; the latter in the bracing mountainous area northward of the Sea of Galilee. *Benjamin* (27), unlike its forefather, became renowned for its warlike qualities (e.g. Judg. 20:15-17; 1 Chron. 8:40;12:1,2).

Joseph, like Judah, receives special attention, althought the description is more personal (22-26; see Deut. 33:13-17). The main themes include: (*a*) *fruitfulness* (22), springing from well-watered roots (see Ps. 1; Jer. 17:7,8); (*b*) *adversity* (23), possibly alluding to Joseph's experiences in Egypt, and inviting comparison with John 15:2, where fruitfulness results from hard pruning; (*c*) *divine enabling* (24), which makes possible the production of the choice fruits of character even through adversity; (*d*) *assurance* (25) – Jacob himself knew that an Almighty God would be to the Joseph tribes what he had personally experienced; (*e*) *separation* (26). The noun Nazirite (see Num. 6) derives from this word which implies a spiritual separation, the foundation for the richest blessing (see 2 Cor. 6:16-18).

Jacob's final request (29,30) was a further affirmation of faith in God's promises.

50 An age closes

Jacob, in death, was accorded special honour, for the period of mourning (3) was only marginally shorter than the seventy-two days prescribed for the death of a Pharaoh. The mummification of the bodies of both Jacob and Joseph (2,3,26) was a practical measure unconnected with the Egyptian view of immortality. Jacob's body was to be taken *immediately* on a long journey; Joseph, with the foresight of faith, arranged for his to *remain* in Egypt until God visited his people in the exodus (24,25). The 'coffin in Egypt' (26) was a token and reminder of this, and Joseph's faith was not overlooked (Exod. 13:19; Josh. 24:32; Heb. 11:22).

Joseph's indirect approach to Pharaoh (4) was caused by his isolation in mourning. It is likely that the magnificent Egyptian escort (7-9), appropriate for a state funeral, remained at Abel-mizraim (10,11), allowing Jacob's family privacy for the final journey to Machpelah (13). This action, incidentally, would reassert their territorial rights in Canaan. The apparently circuitous route to Mamre via Atad (10) may have been prompted by some disorder in Canaan which made a direct approach from the south-west inadvisable, but, in fact, it anticipated the general route taken by Joshua's victorious army.

It is evident that Joseph's brothers continued to live under the shadow of a feared vengeance (15-21). Rejection, slavery and imprisonment formed a seemingly formidable score which might be settled now that Jacob was dead. Joseph was possibly most like Christ in his perfect forgiveness of those who had wronged him, and v.20 exemplifies the truth, 'Man proposes, but God disposes'. Added to forgiveness was a rich provision (21). It is likely that Joseph's tears (17) resulted from his awareness that his brothers' account of Jacob's final charge (16) was a crude fabrication, prompted by the continuing mistrust of a guilty conscience.

Joseph's age at death (22,26) was reckoned, in Egypt, the perfect life span. To see one's grandchildren was likewise regarded as a great blessing. Subsequently Machir was to become the dominant clan in Manasseh (Josh. 17:1); indeed, in Judg. 5:14 it is synonymous with the whole tribe.

THOUGHT: With the deaths of Jacob and Joseph the patriarchal age closes, but the twice-repeated promise 'God will visit you' (24,25) spoke of an assured future.

Questions and themes for further study and discussion on Genesis chapters 46-50

1. Think about the reasons which prompted Joseph to select Goshen as the place of settlement. What factors would influence us in a similar position?

2. In what ways is 47:25 an analogy of Christ's redemptive work?

3. Is there any connection between Jacob's remembrance of Dan's treachery and his interjection (49:17,18)? What is the relationship between trusting God and trusting man?

4. 'Conscience doth make cowards of us all.' How are these words of Shakespeare illustrated in the case of Joseph's brothers? How can we best deal with a guilty conscience?

5. What are the main lessons we may draw from the book of Genesis?

6. 'God will visit you.' Has this promise any relevance for us today?

EXODUS
Introduction

The English title derives from the main Greek version, the Septuagint (LXX). It means 'departure', thus commemorating the central historical event recorded. The Hebrew title, as in many Old Testament books, is taken from the opening words, beginning with a conjunction, 'And these are the names'. G. A. Chadwick regards this as 'a silent indication of truth, that each author was not recording certain isolated incidents, but parts of one great drama, events which joined hands with the past and future, looking before and after'. Certainly there is a close connection between Genesis and Exodus. The promise given to the patriarchs is worked out in measure as Jacob's family is welded, by adversity and divine intervention, into a nation.

Exodus is, pre-eminently, *the book of redemption*, and the imagery derived from events like the Passover, the crossing of the Red Sea, the manna, the rock which Moses struck, and the sacrifices has frequently been applied to God's supreme redemptive activity in Christ. Moses is the great central figure, not merely in Exodus, but of the whole of the Old Testament. In Exodus we see God preparing and using him for his ministry as the deliverer from bondage and mediator of the Old Covenant.

Exodus divides naturally into two main sections. Chapters 1-18 deal with Israel's redemption from Egypt. Chapters 19-40 are concerned with the covenant between God and Israel, the laws which govern it and the worship which accompanies it. Of great importance within this section are: (*a*) the *ten commandments*, one of the basic elements in Israel's relationship with God (20:1-17); (*b*) the *'book of the covenant'* (20:22-23:33; see also 24:3-7), which, coming soon after the departure from Egypt, may be viewed as the prototype and first draft of the entire Torah (Pentateuch). The tradition that Moses wrote the entire book of Exodus dates back at least to the time of Ezra in the late fifth century BC.

For further study, Exodus by H. R. Jones (in the *New Bible Commentary*) and *Exodus* (Tyndale Old Testament Commentary) by Alan Cole are commended.

Analysis of Exodus

1 A cruel bondage

A small beginning (1-7). A comparison with Genesis 46:8-27 shows that of the 'seventy persons' (5), only two, Dinah and Sarah, were females. To this, therefore, must be added the wives and possibly the family servants. Earlier on, Abraham's private army included 318 family retainers when Lot was rescued (Gen. 14:14). This considerable group, together with the fact that the birth rate in deprived groups tends to be higher than in an affluent society, partially accounts for the prodigious increase of v.7. But a *miraculous* increase had been foretold (e.g. Gen. 22:17).

An increasing problem (8-14). Exodus gives no clear indication of chronology, but biblical tradition testifies to a 400-year sojourn in Egypt (Gen. 15:13; Exod. 12:40; Acts 7:6), most of which would fall between verses 6 and 8. The Egyptian dynasty favourable to Joseph's generation is usually identified with the Hyksos rulers (1720–1570 BC), who had strong Semitic connections. The Pharaoh 'who did not know Joseph' (8) was probably Sethos I (1309–1290 BC), who initiated the 19th Dynasty. Sethos and his successor, Ramses II (1290–1224 BC), had extensive building projects in the Nile Delta area, including the store cities noted here (11). Sethos inaugurated a new, tougher line against the Hebrews, viewing the presence of a large alien community as a potential threat (10), although v.9 is probably a relative rather than an absolute statement. This policy would further isolate the Hebrews and strengthen their sense of unity as they suffered this cruel oppression. There is an obvious increase in the severity of this (11-14), a reminder that evil policies, once instituted, tend to become progressively more vicious.

The 'final solution' (15-22). Fear of the increasing Hebrew population, overcoming the awareness of their value as a slave-labour force, climaxed in a policy of elimination. At first, this was controlled through the midwives, whose loyalty to God rightly took precedence over obedience to a manifestly evil law (compare Acts 4:19,20). Their excuse to Pharaoh (19), in the light of v.17, was no more than a half-truth, but their *motive* was obedience to God, and for this they were commended (20). Later on, Pharaoh's edict (22) threw the onus back upon all his subjects, thus involving individual parents and probably his own people, making them direct accomplices in his murderous policies.

THOUGHT: Imagine yourself in the place of the slave-labourer (14), and the father or mother of a new-born son (22). Can you identify as sympathetically with an oppressed, deprived group in today's world? Does Hebrews 4:15-5:2 help determine our attitude?

2 An act that changed history

Pharaoh's harsh decree could have quickly succeeded, since there would soon be no Hebrew males, and the females would quickly have been absorbed as slave wives. It was thwarted by the courageous action of a couple who refused to acquiesce weakly in an immoral policy. Their decisive action, springing from their faith (Heb. 11:23), was the first step in the deliverance not only of their son, but also of their nation. Their plan was realistic and carefully conceived. Moses' parents probably recognised that help could come only through someone like Pharaoh's daughter (5). They probably knew her character and were conversant with her timetable, leaving Miriam, already primed with her suggestion (7), to keep watch. Possibly Pharaoh's daughter realised what was afoot. Moses would enjoy all the privileges of a child of the harem (there were several in Egypt), including a first-class education in either the equivalent of the civil service or the army. The person to deliver Israel must be himself a Hebrew, but how could a member of a slave group gain the requisite diplomatic, administrative and military skills (to mention but three) which such a mission required? The miracle is explained in this section. Moses was later to renounce these considerable privileges (see Heb. 11:24-26), surely because his upbringing under his own mother (9,10) had given him a sense of his true identity. His Egyptian education, however, reflected in all his subsequent achievements, was not wasted.

Moses evidently expected his fellow-Hebrews to accept him as their deliverer (11-15; see Acts 7:25), but his impetuous action, though well meant, was out of God's timing. The long years of his stay in Midian (15-22) were needed, for many necessary lessons were not included in the curriculum of Pharaoh's court. Yet the essential qualities, especially that courage which faced great odds in defence of the helpless, were already evident (17). The almost fairy-story ending (21,22) is qualified by the name given to Gershom – 'a stranger there'. His heart remained with his oppressed people. God, too, did not forget his people as their bondage increased (23-25).

Note: Verse 19, 'An Egyptian'. This would hardly have appeared in a fabrication. Moses' bearing, speech, dress and the presence of Egyptians in nearby copper mines would account for the mistake.

QUESTION: The training as a desert shepherd was as valuable as that in Pharaoh's court. How ready are we to accept training which demands less pleasant surroundings?

3 Encounter with God

Whilst the centre of the Midianite kingdom was east of the Gulf of Aqabah, the Midianites, essentially a nomadic people, were found in a wide area from the Sinai Peninsula to Transjordan (e.g. Judg. 6). The long stay with Jethro in this region would acquaint Moses with its nature and geography, an important preparation for the wilderness period.

Like many biblical characters, Moses encountered God in the normal round of everyday duties (1). The bush, burning but not consumed (2), reminds of Israel's subsequent history, often under fierce persecution but miraculously retaining her identity. The revelation was not to pander to idle curiosity, however, as Moses soon discovered (3). His *first* lesson was that God was holy, and not to be approached irreverently (5). *Secondly,* God underlined the continuity with the past (6,15-17). He was no 'new' God, an important point to bear in mind in interpreting v.14. *Thirdly,* he was deeply involved with Israel (7,8). This is the first use of 'my people', and the verbs 'I have seen . . . heard . . . know . . . come down' reveal him as Israel's champion and anticipate the incarnation. *Fourthly,* the revelation was purposeful (10), involving Moses himself in God's redemptive activity (compare the revelations to Isaiah, Isa. 6, and Paul, Acts 9). Moses' objection, on the basis of his personal inadequacy, was met by the assurance of God's presence (12; see Matt. 28:20).

Finally, Moses learnt something of God's character. This was the purpose of his question (13) since a name, in Scripture, involves the nature of the person. In v.14 the first person singular imperfect of the verb 'to be' is used (Yahweh derives from the corresponding third person singular 'He is' etc.). The verb can be past, present or future, but always involving the sense of continuity. It stresses God's *active* existence, but the very indefiniteness allows an element of inscrutability. The revelation is an *unfolding* one; God will show himself in whatever way he chooses. The name itself was not new. Its shortened form occurs in the name of Moses' mother, Jochebed (6:20), and there is reasonably strong evidence for its extra-biblical use. It received a completely new content, however, at this time.

FOR ENCOURAGEMENT: God knows of difficulties and opposition in advance (19). How does this affect our attitude?

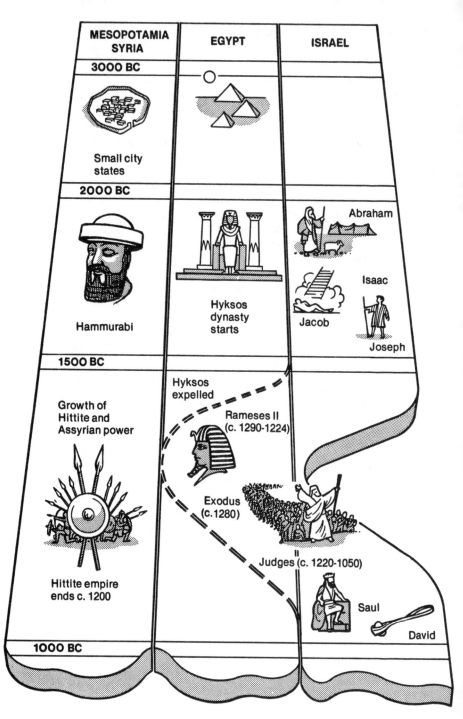

MESOPOTAMIA SYRIA	EGYPT	ISRAEL
3000 BC		
Small city states		
2000 BC		
Hammurabi	Hyksos dynasty starts	Abraham Isaac Jacob Joseph
1500 BC	Hyksos expelled	
Growth of Hittite and Assyrian power	Rameses II (c. 1290-1224) Exodus (c. 1280)	Judges (c. 1220-1050)
Hittite empire ends c. 1200		Saul David
1000 BC		

Alternate date for The Exodus is 1440 BC.

4 The call of God

Moses, probably the greatest figure in the Old Testament, was peculiarly reluctant to accept his commission. Earlier he had objected on the ground of his general unsuitability (3:11); here he shows his fear of rejection (1). As a young man he had set out to be the champion of his downtrodden people, only to be rejected (2:11-14). Clearly the hurt and humiliation of this had lingered. God graciously accommodates himself to Moses, and the first encouragement included two miracles (2-8), with the promise of a third (9). Throughout Scripture there is a 'divine economy' in the use of miracles; they invariably came at transitional points of crisis. There are *four* of these: (*a*) the Exodus period; (*b*) the sharp crisis concerning Baal worship in the days of Elijah and Elisha; (*c*) the Incarnation, and (*d*) the early days when the church was established.

Moses further objected on the score of his lack of eloquence (10; compare, Jer. 1:6). Whilst this was met initially by the provision of his brother, Aaron (14-16), Moses himself became a great orator, as the book of Deuteronomy shows (and Acts 7:22). He was, in fact, making excuses, and his downright *unwillingness* to accept God's challenge at last emerged (13). God's anger (14) is a reminder that, whilst he understands our natural timidity and sense of inadequacy, there comes the point where the refusal of our God-given task is virtually an assertion that he doesn't know what he is about. But again, God demonstrated his long-suffering (14-17).

Moses' continual reluctance is also shown in the partial reason he gave Jethro (18). There was scant delight in his real mission, perhaps understandably, for it was a tough assignment (21). The promised meeting with Aaron (14,27) must have provided further encouragement, showing the Lord's capacity to direct affairs. A man divinely chosen and commissioned, however, cannot escape the demand of complete obedience (24-26). Zipporah's prompt action, and her anger, implies that Moses had been negligent, and God's express command, assumed here, cannot be flouted lightly. However, the general impression which dominates is of God's patience in dealing with his servant, and of his tender concern for his people (22,23,31).

TO THINK THROUGH: God regards me as his child (Heb. 12:5-11).

Questions for further study and discussion on Exodus chapters 1-4

1. To what extent have we a responsibility for the welfare of minority communities in our midst? What practical action is needed in your community?

2. 'Faith shows itself in actions, even in adversity.' Is this *always* true?

3. In view of Israel's plight why did God take so long to prepare Moses for his task? What can we learn from this?

4. Is *anyone* completely adequate for God's work (compare 2 Cor. 3:5,6)?

5. What qualities does God require in those he chooses for leadership?

6. Consider the place of miracles in today's world.

5:1-6:1 Request and reaction

Moses' obedience to God's command (3:18,19) met with the chilling response anticipated. To Pharaoh, God was unknown, hence the element of contempt in his refusal (2). He was soon to discover by bitter experience *who* the Lord was. His main concern was to maintain his grip on his slave-labour force, and the departure of the whole group for a religious ceremony seemed to threaten this. Many scholars accept that a living memory of a pilgrimage festival, here revived by Moses, had remained with the Hebrews during the centuries of their stay in Egypt. Others view the 'three days' journey' (3) as (*a*) a reference to Sinai, but only *Sinn Bishr* in north-west Sinai, or another adjacent peak, could be reached in such a brief period, and even then, only by lightly burdened men. (*b*) A subterfuge on Moses' part, with no intention of ever returning. It is pointed out that Moses later specified that the entire group and all their possessions were involved (10:9), but this may have been a hardening of Moses' attitude after Pharaoh's objection of the earlier, modest request. (*c*) As a vague reference, with the practical concern of clearing Egyptian frontiers, within which animal sacrifice would be impossible (8:25-27).

Pharaoh and God were obviously on a collision course, for self-interest can be a harsh, unyielding master. At first, Pharaoh's counter-measures seemed to be effective. Output was to be maintained, but the straw used to reinforce the bricks was no longer supplied; a considerable economy for Pharaoh (7-9). When, inevitably, production suffered the Hebrew foremen (14) were made the scapegoats. They, in turn, rounded bi.terly on Moses and Aaron (20,21). Pharaoh's aim to crush any spirit of rebellion, and to drive a wedge between Moses and Aaron and their people, had succeeded. The attempt to re-establish worship (8,17) seemed to have rebounded violently. Not only were the two brothers unpopular, but Moses himself, apparently unmindful that God had foretold that Pharaoh would not co-operate (3:19;4:21), erupted in sharp complaint (22,23). Everything seemed to have misfired. But 'man's extremity is God's opportunity'. Pharaoh might appear strong, but when God acted (6:1) it would be irresistible. Ultimately Pharaoh's 'strength' would be devoted to getting rid of the Hebrews, not holding on to them.

QUESTION: When God began to work the situation worsened. How can this fit in with his plan?

6:2-27 Moses recommissioned

Retrospect. As we have observed, the name Yahweh was *not* absolutely new. It occurs in Genesis 4:26 and 22:14, and the view that a later writer substituted this better known name for an original, more widely diffused, name for God is not convincing. As suggested, the probability is that the *character* of the Lord, reflected in his name, received a new development at this time. Support for this comes from a study of Jer. 16:21, where a fresh historical development, revealing new facets of Yahweh's character, connects with an already known name.

Prospect. That character is made clear in the Lord's promises (2-8). He is faithful to his covenant (4,8). One of the main points of the covenant with the patriarchs, the gift of the promised land, is underlined here (see Gen. 15:18-21). In every Israelite 'creed' (e.g. Deut. 6:21-25;26:5-9; Josh. 24:2-13) reference is made to this aspect of the promise to the patriarchs. But the name Yahweh is, from the period of Moses onwards, *the* name which is particularly connected with the covenant relationship – other names tend to fall into the background. Apart from its localised use in Gen. 48:16, the word 'redeem' is found for the first time (6) – Exodus shows the Lord pre-eminently as the God of *redemption*. Involved in all this is the wondrously close *relationship* he envisages with his people (7; see 19:5,6; Deut. 4:32-35). Israel, however, crushed by cruel bondage and disappointed hopes, failed to respond (9), and Moses himself appears utterly dejected (12). God's promises, however, are not necessarily thwarted by human failure and apathy, for he is a God of infinite understanding (Ps. 103:13,14; Isa. 40:28). Moses is directed to approach Pharaoh with more exacting terms than before (13, compare 3:19).

Continuity for the future (14-25). The list is not comprehensive; it includes only Jacob's three oldest sons. Its principal interest is the tribe of Levi and the family of Aaron, i.e. the *priestly* line.

Notes: (*a*) Two items in this chapter would hardly appear in a fabrication: (*1*) the way in which Moses, the great leader, was so easily discouraged; (*2*) the fact that Amram married his aunt (20), which was forbidden in the law of Moses (Lev. 18:12). (*b*) The genealogy is probably selective since the four generations noted could hardly have spanned 120 years, let alone 430 (12:40).

THOUGHT: God's promises are not thwarted by human failure and apathy, for he is a God of infinite understanding.

6:28-7:24 Confrontation

The narrative, interrupted by the genealogy of 6:14-27, is now resumed. Moses' last objection (30) is met by the assurance that he would have God's word, which more than compensates for human weakness. On the surface, there is an incredible temerity in the suggestion that Moses would appear divine to Pharaoh, contacting him through an intermediary (1,2), but in fact Egypt's ruler *was* to cower abjectly before the brothers (10:16,17). In conjunction with 4:16, this section is highly important for our understanding of the role of the prophet in Israel. Fundamentally he was to be God's 'mouth' or spokesman, announcing his will.

Pharaoh's hardness of heart has been viewed as a problem (3,13,14,22, compare 4:21). Three types of reference alternate: that God hardened Pharaoh's heart; that Pharaoh hardened his heart; and the 'neutral' statement that Pharaoh's heart was hardened. Pharaoh's response nowhere suggests the action of an automaton (see 5:2). It would be legitimate, by modern standards, to account for it in terms of human psychology – Pharaoh was so conditioned by his unrelenting opposition that ultimately he was not able to act out of character or change his mind. True natural law, however, is part of God's ordering and control of this universe, an expression of his being. Hebrew understanding, with its emphasis upon God's sovereignty, bypassed 'secondary' causes and often attributed events and attitudes directly to God (see 1 Sam. 16:14; 1 Kings 22:20-23).

The two preliminary miracles (8-12,17-22) were both counterfeited by the 'secret arts' (11) of Egypt's magicians. They may have employed sleight of hand or hypnosis of some kind to make a serpent as rigid as a rod. Verse 24, suggesting that the impurities which contaminated the Nile could be filtered out, may indicate that the Nile was blood-like in colour and texture rather than actual blood (compare Joel 2:31). It could also explain how Egypt's sorcerers were able to duplicate the miracle. Commentators frequently point out that the majority of the plagues can be explained rationally, assuming that an initial, unusually severe, inundation of the Nile involved a high degree of pollution. Even if this is the case it by no means eliminates the miraculous element; in each case the timing was meticulous, and the majority of the plagues were announced beforehand.

QUESTION: Does God work today through natural phenomena?

7:25-8:32 Continued conflict

The time reference (7:25) suggests that God did not act too quickly; he allowed Pharaoh time for reflection. Indeed, if the first plague involved an unusually severe annual rise in the level of the Nile (which occurred about July or August), and the final plague was at Passover time, the whole sequence of plagues covered about seven or eight months.

Plague two – frogs (2-15). Many of the plagues seem directed against the impotent gods of Egypt. The Nile itself was sacred, and the frog was connected with the gods Hapi and Hekt, particularly as a symbol of fertility. The pollution of the Nile could have compelled frogs to leave the river in vast numbers, and the piles of rotting frogs (14) would certainly have provided the breeding grounds for the plagues of gnats and flies. The Egyptian magicians only worsened the situation by their ability to duplicate this miracle, but they could do nothing to remove the menace. It was to Moses and Aaron that Pharaoh appealed (8). God's sovereignty was underlined in the precise timing of the deliverance (10), as it was also in the complete exclusion of the flies from the land of Goshen (22). Pharaoh's insincerity throughout this chapter (15,32) demonstrates the need for a change of heart – Prov. 26:23 is an apt commentary on his attitude.

Plague three – gnats (16-19). The exact nature of this plague is disputed; it could also have been mosquitoes, fleas or sandflies. All four produce considerable personal discomfort. For the first time the magicians are unable to parallel the miracle. Grudgingly, they admitted the higher power (19) that *they*, if not Pharaoh, must have recognised much earlier.

Plague four – flies (20-24). The word used suggests that various types of flies were involved. The further impact of this plague compelled Pharaoh's partial submission (25). Whilst sacrifice was not unknown in Egypt, the Hebrew customs would certainly have revolted the Egyptians. In the late fifth century, when the Jewish temple at Elephantine (*Yeb*) was destroyed by rioting Egyptians, animal sacrifice was one of the issues involved. Note how Moses' good faith contrasts with Pharaoh's duplicity, of which Moses was fully aware (29-32).

QUESTION: How does Ecclesiastes 5:4 relate to Pharaoh and ourselves?

9 The conflict escalates

Plague five – cattle plague (1-7). The earlier plagues would infect the low-lying pastures where the cattle were grazed after the seasonal inundation. References like Deut. 28:60 show how susceptible the Nile Delta area was to outbreaks of various plagues. A comparison of vs.3,6, and 19-21 suggests that not all the cattle had been put out to pasture. Once more, a miracle is emphasised by a prior announcement and a strictly limited area affected. Pharaoh appears curious rather than concerned (7).

Plague six – boils (8-12). This came without warning and was probably caused by the same combination of factors which led to the cattle plague. The account stresses the complete impotence of the magicians, now amongst the principal sufferers (11).

Plague seven – hail (13-35). For the first time human life is involved, and the greater detail signifies the sharpening of the conflict as Pharaoh's attitude becomes increasingly rigid. Moses is instructed to set out clearly the principles involved (14-17), and a merciful concern provides both warning *and advice* (19). Division is introduced into the Egyptian ranks as opportunity is given for the more discerning and less stubborn to escape (20,21). Note how this involved an element of faith on *their* part akin to that of Noah (Gen. 7:7,10), for the hail had not yet come. Presumably many of these Egyptians would be amongst the 'mixed multitude' which accompanied Moses into the wilderness (12:38). An exceptionally violent and terrifying thunderstorm, unusual in Egypt, is indicated (23-25,28). Pharaoh's apparently frank admission of guilt (27) was prompted more by fear than by a radical change of heart, as Moses was quick to see (30). Unfortunately for Pharaoh, his hardened attitude increased the terror to the point where he *was* really willing to let Israel go, without qualification (compare 28).

Note: Verses 31,32 add to the time-reference, indicating January in a normal agricultural year.

QUESTION: 'Moses' prayer could open (or close!) the heavens but could not open the heart of a self-willed man' (J. Clement Connell). How far is this true?

10 Impasse

Plague eight – locusts (1-20). 'A plague of locusts is one of the most feared of all catastrophes in the East; it usually destroys in the shortest time imaginable every green thing that grows, and results in dreadful famine' (Martin Noth). No wonder that Pharaoh's servants, alarmed at their master's obduracy, and concerned that the land should be spared complete devastation, found the courage to protest (7). Pharaoh's reactions show how hardened he had become, and how desperately he sought some justification for his attitude. Although Moses had, throughout, indicated that the whole nation was involved, Pharaoh now sought to limit the exodus to men only (11), accusing the Hebrews of some ulterior motive (10).

Occasionally in the Old Testament, the *means* of a miracle is made clear (13,19), which by no means explains it away (e.g. 14:21). If locusts are to travel any distance they need wind assistance, since their natural range is limited. Again, the timing of the arrival and departure of these voracious insects was immaculate. Pharaoh's confession (16,17) *seems* sincere, but once more it proved completely superficial: when the emergency was over his repentance and promises evaporated.

Plague nine – thick darkness (21-29). It has been observed that the first nine plagues can be grouped in triads of increasing severity, with the last in each group, the third, the sixth, and the ninth, being unannounced. This plague, involving no physical hurt or damage, may appear an anticlimax, but the impact of fearful anticipation must have been considerable. Ra, the sun god, and one of Egypt's principal deities, had been completely eclipsed. Pharaoh's apparent concession (24) was, in fact, valueless, for how could Israel sacrifice to the Lord without sacrificial beasts? Moses points this out with firmness as well as irony (25,26), but relationships between the two men had reached the point where there was no room left to manoeuvre. It was Pharaoh who broke off negotiations with an ultimatum which amounted to a downright rejection of Moses *and* the Lord. It precipitated the final escalation in the series of plagues, and Pharaoh's humiliating 'climb-down' (12:31,32), his threat unfulfilled. Instead of the shadow of death being upon Moses, it was to be upon Pharaoh's household and, tragically, upon every Egyptian family, willingly or unwillingly involved in his rebellious spirit.

QUESTION: Does sin always involve others?

Questions for further study and discussion on Exodus chapters 5-10

1. Consider the relationship between 'management' and 'labour' in Exodus ch.5 in comparison with today's industrial scene. How should Christian principles affect the latter?

2. What other biblical names for God indicate his character?

3. What were Moses' strong and weak points as a negotiator? What is their relevance for us in a different situation?

4. How can we reconcile God's sovereignty with man's godless actions and policies?

5. How long should we continue to negotiate with people we know to be deceitful? Apply this to current national and international issues.

6. 'When we rebel against the Lord it is we who suffer most' (comment on Isa. 1:5,6). Illustrate this from your own experience. Is it always true?

7. Is it true that God is always on the side of the oppressed, as one modern school of thought believes? What is God's concern for justice and how should his people embody it?

11 Parting of the ways

This chapter completes the previous one and begins to set the scene for the final encounter. It is likely that vs.1-3 deal with a situation before the ninth plague, since it appears that Moses was in the presence of his own people, not Pharaoh (2), and the final plague is not yet specified (1). Preparations are thus set in motion for Israel's departure from Egypt, which would not be empty-handed. The suggestion that the Hebrews were urged to be deceitful, borrowing from the Egyptians but not returning, is far-fetched and unnecessary. Only partially relevant to the actual situation is the point, often made, that the Egyptian gifts would be but poor compensation for generations of slave labour. Undoubtedly some Egyptians would be grateful for the consideration shown in 9:19-21, and there was evidently an unusual spirit of generosity towards the Hebrews (3,12:35,36). However, the desperation caused by the final plague would mean that any price would be paid to get rid of Israel.

Verses 4-8 continue Moses' interview with Pharaoh, as v.8b shows. The final, awful catastrophe which would subdue Pharaoh's stubborn will was clearly announced, although the specific day was not made clear. An absolute minimum of four days, allowing the necessary preparation for the Passover (12:3,6), was to intervene before the final blow. We can imagine the sense of dreadful anticipation; after all, Moses' other threats had been fulfilled to the letter. Up to this point Egypt had been reasonably united behind their revered monarch (but see 10:7). Now they would be jolted into independent action (8).

So the last appeal to Pharaoh ended abruptly, with strong feeling on both sides (8; see 10:28). Verses 9 and 10 summarise the whole series of negotiations.

QUESTION: In what sense did Moses display righteous anger? Is there a place for this in our lives? What are the attendant dangers?

12:1-28 Provision for remembrance

In a sense the first Passover (1-13) marked the birth-day of Israel; note the first use of the description 'congregation of Israel' (3,6). Passover was also the distinctive, most important Israelite feast, celebrating God's sovereignty in history. In the period of the monarchy, it was Tabernacles that became *the* great popular feast, the beginning of the civil and religious year. But significantly, the two great reforming kings, Hezekiah and Josiah, both made Passover central in their reformed order (2 Kings 23:21-23; 2 Chron. 30). After the Exile, partially under Babylonian influence, the Jewish year was altered to begin in the Spring, at Passover. There is evidence that Passover was celebrated in some way before the Exodus, possibly at the lambing season, when a nomadic people journeyed to their spring pastures. Details like the carrying of a staff, the wearing of sandals, the girt loins, the food quickly prepared, eaten and cleared away, and the incidence of the full moon to facilitate travelling, support this. In any case, Passover was completely transformed by its historical connections with the Exodus.

Other important considerations are: (*a*) the principle of true sacrifice (5) – only the best is good enough for God (compare Mal. 1:13,14). The Passover lamb foreshadowed the Lamb of God (Heb. 7:26;9:14; 1 Pet. 1:19). (*b*) The sense of fellowship (4). It was impossible to be lonely at Passover time. The feast was celebrated in families or neighbourhoods, ten males being the minimum number. (*c*) The completeness of the feast (10) suggests the completion of God's redemptive activity. (*d*) There is a twofold stress, on communion *and expiation*, witnessed by the sprinkling of blood as a sin offering (7,22,23). (*e*) The fact that *all* partook, regardless of ceremonial defilement, contrasts markedly with future observances of the feast. (*f*) The need for faith is apparent. The procedure of vs.21-23 might appear ridiculous, but it was literally a life or death affair. Only where faith issued in obedience was there deliverance.

Connected intimately with Passover was the Feast of Unleavened Bread (14-20) which, in the agricultural year, marked the beginning of the barley harvest. It signified a complete break with the past, indicated by the eradication of anything leavened, and a new beginning. It thus reinforced an important aspect of the Exodus event.

QUESTION: What do vs.26,27 (compare 13:8,14; Deut. 6:20-25) tell us about the importance of educating our children?

12:29-51 The Exodus

At the hour predicted (11:4) the final, devastating blow fell. Imagination can supply the details; Scripture simply notes the 'great cry' (30). J. C. Rylaarsdam comments, 'The *great cry* of anguish (see 11:6) symbolises the complete disintegration of human pride at the appearance of the day of wrath (compare Isa. 2:12-22; Joel 2:6)'. Significantly, Pharaoh made an immediate, urgent appeal to the brothers (30-32), pocketing his pride (compare 10:28) in the light of this catastrophe. It was God's judgement upon him for his evil nature and policies; a judgement, too, upon his people, most of whom had willingly implemented his harsh, heartless decrees. We must assume that a minority of more humane Egyptians were unfortunately involved. Observe the stress, in Exodus, on God's absolute sovereignty. A self-willed, hard-hearted monarch sought to impose his own authority, but his obduracy only made his inevitable submission the more painful and humiliating (compare Acts 26:14).

The first leg of the Exodus, to Succoth (37), a distance of about twenty-five miles, was without any major halt (see 39). Succoth lay west of the present Lake Timsah, and south-south-east of Ramses (1:11). Clearly Moses was deliberately avoiding the closely guarded main coastal road to the promised land (compare 13:17,18). The numbers involved seem high and scholars usually admit the biblical evidence that Israel was a relatively small group (compare 23:28-30), with an effective fighting force of about 40,000 (Josh. 4:13; Judg. 5:8). Such an attitude does not seek to explain away the miraculous; indeed, a vast number would lessen the miracle which the Lord worked for an *insignificant* people (compare Deut. 7:7). The precise figure of 430 years (40) corresponds with the round figure of Genesis 15:13 (compare Acts 7:6). It was remarkable that an alien element within Egypt: (*a*) retained its identity during succeeding phases of prosperity and adversity; (*b*) was so slightly influenced by the advanced Egyptian culture. The only plausible explanation is that the Hebrews already possessed strong traditions.

The Passover was open, without distinction, to *all* those circumcised who earnestly wished to keep it (43-49). This legislation was probably prompted by the fact of the 'mixed multitude' (38), sometimes a source of weakness, and yet an indication of the attractiveness of Israel's faith in an all-powerful God.

QUESTION: What reasonable restriction ought to be applied to *our* feast of remembrance (1 Cor. 11:23-32)?

13 'The Lord brought you out'

The law of the first-born (1-16). The earlier legislation, given to Moses and Aaron and delivered in the first instance to the elders (12:21), is repeated to the whole multitude, presumably at the end of the first day's journey. Moses takes the bare command (2) and amplifies it against the great deliverance wrought by God. Obedience becomes a delight when gratitude is in the heart. The spiritual connections worked out here, *and* in the New Testament (e.g. Rom. 12:1,2), are (*a*) deliverance, (*b*) remembrance and (*c*) dedication. The Israelites had been spared the fate of Egypt's first-born; henceforth the first-born were to be dedicated to God. A few scholars suggest that this legislation replaces an earlier custom of sacrificing the first-born, but there is no evidence for such a practice. The sense of gratitude for a historical deliverance, and the more general principle that God, the 'Author and Giver of all good things', merits our choicest gifts in response, are sufficient explanation. Numbers 3:40-51 complements this legislation, and shows how seriously it was taken. The tribe of Levi was set apart in place of first-born Israelites, and the small number not covered by the precise number of Levites had to be individually redeemed at five shekels each.

Note again the stress on education (8,14), and grateful, continual remembrance (9). Verses 9 and 16 were not intended to be followed in a literal, physical way (compare Deut. 6:6-9;11:18-21), but at a later date all male Jews, when at prayer, wore small leather containers (phylacteries) attached to the forehead and left wrist. Other similar containers (mezuzah), also holding excerpts of Scripture, were attached to the doorpost and religiously touched when entering or leaving. Man invariably finds the observance of the letter of the law easier than its spirit.

Journeyings of an infant nation (17-22). Israel might appear equipped for battle (18), but initially the people needed careful shielding. God kept them from obvious danger (17,18) and provided a physical manifestation of his presence, giving assurance as well as guidance (21,22). The bones of Joseph (19; see Gen. 50:25; Josh. 24:32; Heb. 11:22) would further remind them of his personal response of faith to the future of his people.

QUESTION: What provision has God made for encouraging and guiding his followers today?

14 'The Lord fights for them'

Pharaoh's pursuit (1-9). The place names (2) have not been firmly identified, but most scholars set the great deliverance from the pursuing Egyptians south of Lake Timsah, or between the two Bitter Lakes, in the reedy, relatively shallow extension of the Red Sea. 'Turn back' (2) may indicate that the Israelites came against Egyptian fortifications (Migdol means 'watch-tower'). The tension between Pharaoh's apparently free actions (5-7) and the statements of vs.4 and 8 is explained by the divine foreknowledge. Memory, even when painful, can be short-lived, and Pharaoh's realisation that his slave labour force had disappeared overcame the fear generated by the recent evidences of God's power. He kept the departing Israelites under surveillance (3), and their uncertain progress may have encouraged him to attack.

The Lord's victory (10-31). The narrative has every mark of authenticity. No nation would have invented a tradition which presented its ancestors in such a shameful light! There was no faith in their cry to the Lord (10), as their bitter complaint to Moses shows (11,12). Evidently they had forgotten, temporarily, the solid indications of God's power in the preceding months. But 'let him who is without (this) sin among you be the first to throw a stone' (John 8:7). Moses, too, had cried to the Lord (15), but his prayer was one of supremely confident trust (13,14; compare 2 Chron. 20:15-17). God's deliverance, in fact, involved more than the passive faith of Moses' 'stand firm' (13). Israel was to 'go forward', between the banked-up waters, no small act of faith, even though the alternatives were death or the resumption of slavery. God used the same force of nature as in the plague of locusts (21; compare 10:13), and with the same perfect timing. Later, among the nations who worshipped the personified powers of nature, this incident and others would demonstrate that Yahweh was sovereign in nature as well as history. The 'morning watch' (24), between 2 and 6 am, indicates a night crossing, with the howling east wind and the Passover moon adding to an unforgettable experience (see Ps. 77:14-20). With Israel safely across the wind abated and the waters returned at the divine command (26), destroying the flower of the Egyptian army. Pharaoh's contemptuous question (5:2) had been decisively answered, and Israel's faith was immeasurably strengthened by this fresh experience of God's grace (31).

MEDITATION: 'What sort of man is this, that even winds and sea obey him?'(Matt. 8:27).

The route of the Exodus

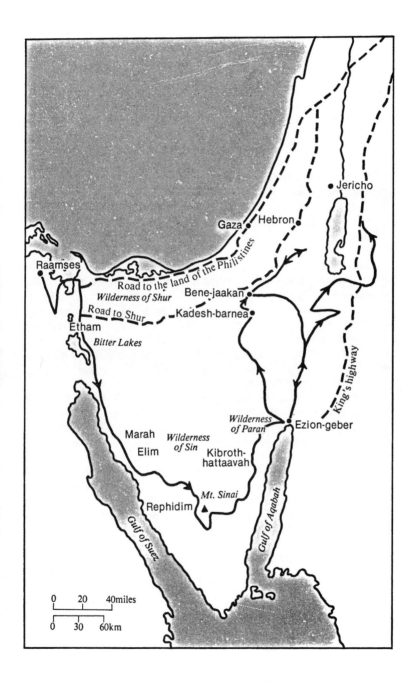

15 Redemption Praise

The Song of Moses (1-18), like the Song of Deborah (Judg. 5), was composed spontaneously, and so displays a natural vigour and strength. The admittedly archaic features of the poem support this early date. Poetry, for the average westerner, is not a normal mode of expression. The incidence of poetry, in the Psalter and Prophets, for example, shows how natural it was in Israel.

It is almost impertinent to analyse something which sprang so readily from the heart. But see how a new-found, personal experience of God's redemption *should* find expression. The hyperbolic element has been criticised but how can God's power ever be adequately described? The practical monotheism of v.11 is also important. The non-existence of other gods is not demonstrated at this stage of Israel's development, but her God, Yahweh, so dominates the world-stage that no room is left for rivals.

If the verbs of vs.13-18 be regarded as prophetic perfects, in which future events are spoken of as fulfilled, a device which reflects the *certainty* attaching to God's promises, then this, too, is part of the Song. But since vs.13 and 17 appear to refer to Solomon's Temple on Mt. Zion (e.g. compare Pss. 78:68,69;87:1-3), and since Philistia (14) did not become a kingdom until c.1200–1180 BC, some scholars regard this as a later addition. The probability is that they were original, since they depict the logical outcome of God's redemption. Possibly minor adjustments were made later.

Sadly, the people redeemed (13) and purchased (16), who had voiced their thanksgiving so powerfully, soon lapsed. Grumbling, one of the signs of spiritual immaturity, since whilst it is directed overtly at a person (here Moses, 24; see 16:8), it inevitably involves a *criticism* of God, was characteristic of Israel – twelve times or more she was guilty of this. There are many, well-authenticated instances of the use of a particular bush or plant to neutralise bitterness or acidity in drinking water. God *could* have effected this miracle directly, without any other agency, but frequently he invites man's co-operation, in faith.

Note: Verse 20. Miriam, 'the sister of *Aaron'* (rather than Moses), is so called probably because Moses was absent from their home in Egypt. Her song (21) repeats the first couplet of v.1; possibly it was longer originally.

THOUGHT: God frequently invites man's co-operation, in faith.

Questions for further study and discussion on Exodus chapters 11-15

1. What was the source of Moses' greatness (11:3)? How does this connect with Num. 12:3? How far is it still a recipe for true greatness?

2. Is faith still important in the God-man relationship? How should it be expressed?

3. Consider the connections between the Passover and the Christian's 'feast of remembrance'.

4. What part should education have in the life of the Christian family and in the life of the Christian Church?

5. Ought the Hebrews to have been ready (compare 12:39; Matt. 25:1-13) in the light of the promised exodus? What expectations do we have for which we remain unprepared?

6. 'The life redeemed must surely be dedicated' (compare Rom. 12:1,2). What comment would you make about this? How does our dedication reveal itself?

7. In what sense was Israel 'baptised into Moses' (1 Cor. 10:2)?

8. What can we learn from Moses and Miriam in ch.15? What ways of celebrating God's delivering acts are appropriate for the Christian?

16 Daily bread

The place names mentioned (15:22,23,27;16:1;17:1) have been variously identified, and much depends on whether Mt. Sinai was the objective of the three days' journey into the wilderness (8:27; compare 3:12). A distance of about fifty to sixty miles would be indicated, which would rule out the traditional site, *Jebel Musa*, which was approximately 200 miles distant. The Israelites, including children, the aged, flocks and herds would travel *much* more slowly (compare 1;12:6). One set of identifications, linked with a suggested site of Sinai, *Sinn Bishr* in north-west Sinai, identifies Marah with the present-day *Bir el Murah* (Bitter Well), east of the port of Suez. Elim would then be *Ayun Musa* (the Springs of Moses), an oasis with twelve wells, some seven miles from Marah. Rephidim, which is specifically connected with Horeb/Sinai (17:1,6), would be in the *Wadi Suder* which leads to *Sinn Bishr*, itself about fifty-five miles from where the Red Sea was crossed. One supporting point is that Rithmah, the third halting-place after Sinai (Num. 33:18), has been identified about twelve miles from *Sinn Bishr*, on the way to the promised land.

The murmuring of the people at Elim was on the issue of food; note how attractive even Egypt seemed from this perspective (3). God, whose forbearance with the immature nation was monumental, met this with the provision of quails and manna. Both could have a natural explanation. The quails, exhausted from their migratory flight over the Red Sea, could be caught in great numbers; but again, there was a perfection in timing. Presumably this was an irregular source of food, since it was repeated later (Num. 11:4-6, 31-34). The continuing supply was the manna. Some have identified it with the edible secretions, normally seasonal, of a number of desert shrubs, e.g. the tamarisk. The miraculous element in the supply included: (*a*) the continuity over two generations; (*b*) the amount necessary for the staple food; (*c*) its non-availability on the Sabbath and (*d*) its abrupt cessation (Josh. 5:11,12). The need for faith, obedience, moderation, consideration and diligence are all observable in the regulations for collecting and using the manna, and formed part of God's training of his people.

Note: Verse 29, *the Sabbath*. There is no positive evidence for Sabbath observance before the Exodus. This section anticipates 20:8-11. Other biblical evidence (e.g. Neh. 9:14; Ezek. 20:12,20) shows that the Sabbath was God's covenant-gift, given at Sinai, although its basis was God's rest after creation (Gen. 2:1-3).

17 Two more crises

Water from the rock (1-7). The Israelites were fast reaching that dangerous position of beginning to *expect* miracles, even to the point of demanding them, whilst remaining basically unimpressed by successive evidences of God's power (compare John 6:25-31). Again they complained (2), and this time there was an ominous edge to their murmuring, with the threat of mob violence of which stoning was an obvious customary expression in such an area (compare 1 Sam. 30:6). Their lack of faith is perhaps more significant as it occurred in the very region where God was to reveal himself as their great covenant-God (6). The elders (5) would be responsible witnesses of this miracle, able not only to report but to encourage faith.

Some scholars view Num. 20:2-13 as a duplicate of this miracle, so it is worth reading to note the considerable variations between the two accounts. Regrettably, Israel was true to human nature in its chronic inability to learn by experience. More than one place bore the name Massah (Proof) and Meribah (Strife), names which became proverbial for Israel's hardness of heart and lack of faith (Deut. 6:16;9:22;33:8; Ps. 95:8).

The second military crisis – encounter with Amalek (8-16). The Amalekites were related to the Edomites (Gen. 36:12). They roamed the semi-desert areas to the south and south-west of Canaan, and in a region of water-scarcity would see Israel as a threat to their existence. Possibly Israel's abundant water supply at this juncture invited this attack, although Deut. 25:17-19 suggests prolonged, cowardly attacks upon straggling Israelites and throws light on the apparently harsh statements of vs.14,16.

Already Joshua, as the military commander, was being groomed for future leadership (compare 14). Later on in Israel's organisation, the *host*, or tribal levies, provided the national army, but with inexperience so widespread at this stage Joshua's army was hand-picked (9). The main point of the incident, however, is that intercession played a more effective part in the victory than did military strategy (compare 2 Chron. 20). The uplifted hands symbolised the divine power directed to a specific situation. Hur, who with Aaron played a minor yet significant part, is mentioned again in 24:14. Josephus, the Jewish historian, distinguishes him as the husband of Miriam.

18 A man of discretion

Relationships (1-12). Jethro would quickly have heard of Egypt's humiliation, and Amalek's defeat, and 3:12 indicated the obvious rendezvous. Moses' dependants had probably been sent back (2) for safety reasons, allowing Moses greater mobility during the negotiations with Pharaoh. Nevertheless, there is a distinct impression that the marriage was not ideal. The name of Moses' first-born, Gershom (Heb. *ger* means sojourner) suggests his loneliness, although the resurgence of faith is indicated in Eliezer's name ('God is my help'). Zipporah's last words before their parting (which is not recorded) were not exactly cordial (4:24-26). Moses' sister, Miriam, rather than Zipporah, emerged as the leader of the women, and Joshua appears much closer to Moses than either of his two sons, neither of whom apparently assumed any responsibility.

However, Moses' relationship with his father-in-law shows a warm, mutual regard. Jethro (1), on the analogy of 1 Sam. 1:9, may have been Midian's leading priest. Moses, as the younger, treated him with appropriate respect (7; compare e.g. 1 Tim. 5:1,17-20). The view that it was Jethro who first introduced Moses to the worship of Yahweh finds scant support here, for Jethro seems surprised at what Yahweh had done (11). Note how the Lord is isolated from all other gods by his mighty deeds, anticipating that monotheism which accepts that there are *no* other gods.

The appointment of judges (13-27). Moses appears as the patriarch of the newly independent community. To administer every aspect of justice imposed an impossible load upon him and doubtless led to irritating delays (compare 2 Sam. 15:1-4). Jethro's criticism was well-founded and his advice sound; moreover, it was advanced in humility, with the recognition that God's endorsement was vital (23, compare 19). The whole structure of Israel's Law is anticipated here, with Moses as the divinely-led architect, yet with others involved in its implementation. Deut. 1:13-18, amplifying this, suggests that the tribes chose their own representatives to the judiciary, which would promote local confidence. Note the stress on qualities of moral excellence (21) as well as native ability. Moses himself formed a 'High Court' for exceptional cases (22; compare Num. 9:6-8). The ultimate aim is well expressed (20b), since Law (Heb. *torah*) originally meant 'direction'.

QUESTION: How important is wise delegation in the service of Christ? Why do many of us find it so hard?

19 Prelude

Jewish tradition links the Feast of Weeks (Pentecost), coming fifty days after Passover, with the giving of the Law at Sinai, which accords with the reference in v.1. They were to stay in this place of revelation, instruction and preparation for almost a year (Num. 10:11), an indication of the importance of this period. Sinai was not a mere staging post; it was the first of Israel's two great goals, the second being the promised land. Unfortunately, the obedience promised in the enthusiasm of the moment (8) was sadly lacking, subsequently resulting in a delay of thirty-eight years before the second goal was attained, and the exclusion of the entire male adult population except Joshua and Caleb (Num. 14:22-24,28-32). God is to be taken seriously. He is holy and majestic, and the relationship with him cannot be entered into 'lightly or inadvisedly'. Verses 4-6 are vital for an understanding of the covenant. They speak of God's redeeming activity, free choice and tender care, the analogy of the eagle illustrating the strength and security which Israel enjoyed (compare Deut. 32:11,12). They were his 'own possession', a word often used of Israel, present or future, and transferred naturally to the church as the spiritual Israel (Deut. 7:6;14:2;26:18; Mal. 3:17; Tit. 2:14; 1 Pet. 2:9). Wherever there is privilege, however, there is also responsibility; the phrase 'a kingdom of priests and a holy nation' (6), whilst hinting at an equal right of approach to God (compare the New Testament doctrine of the 'priesthood of all believers'), has the prior meaning of a nation *set apart* for *responsible* service in a priestly, mediating ministry for the whole world. Early in the Old Testament (compare Gen. 12:3) a form of universalism can be seen. This is not a universalism which insists that all will be saved – but a recognition that God's concern is for the whole world and his grace is available for all.

God's being was carefully safeguarded at Sinai, for his holiness precluded any presumption (10-15). The requirement of sexual abstinence (15) contrasts with the Canaanite fertility cults, where ritual prostitution of both sexes was a regular feature. Israel had to learn from the outset that a holy God required a holy people. As well as the fearful, outward accompaniments of God's majesty and holiness (16-20) there was a final clear warning (21-24). This was one lesson which Israel *did* heed (see 20:18,19).

Note: Verses 22,24. Although the Levitical regulations concerning the priesthood were still to come, the presence of *priests* at this stage shows that the Hebrews already possessed their own developed religious structure.

20:1-7 God speaks

Verses like 31:18 and 34:1 show that the ten commandments were isolated from all other legislation, which was mediated through Moses. The 'ten words' came directly from God and form the decisive element in the covenant relationship. Scholars have recognised that the *form* here follows the well-established pattern of the Hittite (the great 'world-power' in the second-millennium BC) suzerainty treaties. These begin by introducing the great king ('I am the Lord your God'), continue with the recital of his mighty deeds (e.g. 'who brought you out of the land of Egypt'), followed by the various provisions to be observed. The parallels in ch.34 and Josh. 24 strengthen the view that the covenant form goes back to Moses and is not a later development.

The type of law, too, is significant, introduced as each one is by 'You shall . . . You shall not'. There is, in the ancient world, no known parallel to this type of law (known as apodeictic or apodictic), resting solely on God's command without any explanation or qualification – a reminder that God *demands* our absolute, unquestioning obedience. The ten commandments express his character and define his requirements. Another relevant fact is that the tablets on which the commandments were inscribed were placed in the ark, itself situated under the mercy-seat, the 'throne' of the invisible God, in the holy of holies (25:21). In a special way this vital part of the law was under his protection.

The context of the law is God's redemptive acts for Israel (2), for gratitude should lead to loyal obedience. The command to give exclusive allegiance to God alone is not explicitly monotheistic (3); neither does it assert the objective existence of other gods. It is best described as practical monotheism, with a total concentration upon the one, all-powerful, all-gracious God. Since he is so distinct no representation of him was to be made (4,5). In this we meet another unique element; in contrast with the heathen world, with its multiplicity of idols, Israel's religion was to be 'imageless'. Later on, under the pressure of Canaanite religion, Israel was often disobedient to the provisions of Sinai but on this issue the evidence is clear; no representation of a male Israelite deity has yet been discovered. The third commandment (7) was directed against false oaths, magical practices and spiritism. God's name, representative of his character, was not to be treated lightly by association with any of these malpractices.

20:8-26 The other commandments

The traditional Protestant arrangement links the first four command-ments as a summary of man's obligations towards God, and the final six as expressing his duty towards his neighbour. Others prefer a more symmetrical five/five arrangement, arguing that the fifth commandment (12) should be included in the first group because of the special sanctity attaching to parenthood, as the source of human life and the reflection of the authority of God. There is also no universal agreement as to the extent of the individual commandments. Whilst most would accept that v.3 is the first, Jewish traditional scholarship views v.2a as the first commandment, *not* as prologue, but preserves the tenfold arrangement by linking vs.3-6 as the second commandment.

These are relatively minor points when compared with the impor-tance of the 'ten-words' in determining fundamental relationships. It is significant that those connected with God come first, for our attitude to him determines our relationship with others. The transition from God to general relationships *via the family* is likewise a natural one. Whilst there is an emphasis upon outward actions, the final commandment (17) shows that inward attitudes were not overlooked, a point developed further by Christ (Matt. 5:21,22,27,28). The biblical estimate of the Law's value is well expressed by Paul (Rom. 7:12), but Jeremiah, followed by Ezekiel (Jer. 31:31-34; Ezek. 36:25-27), saw that its essential weakness was in its outwardness. Man, in his weakness, needs an inward dynamic and incentive which was brought by Christ's redeem-ing sacrifice and the gift of the Holy Spirit. Israel, in spite of their fear on this occasion (18-20), soon forgot (ch.32; compare Ps. 106:21).

The book of the covenant (20:22-23:33; compare 24:7) is of great importance, as the solemn ceremony of ratification makes clear (24:1-11). It may be regarded as the nucleus of the entire Pentateuch. It begins by reinforcing the earlier commandments (22,23). Altars were to be simple, not elaborate (24,25), and any possibility of indecent exposure was to be eliminated (26). *Nothing* must be allowed to detract from the altar as the symbol of man's need and God's grace. Nor were altars to be erected indiscriminately; they were at sites chosen and honoured by God (24).

QUESTION: What is the relationship between the two types of fear in v.20?

Questions for further study and discussion on Exodus chapters 16-20

1. 'Give us this day our daily bread' (Matt. 6:11). Are there connections between this petition and the giving of the manna (16:13-36)? Bearing in mind modern methods of food production, what does this mean for us?

2. Consider the significance of the name 'The Lord is my banner' (or 'sign', Exod. 17:15).

3. We often say 'prayer changes things'. What do we mean? How does the statement relate to our belief in a Sovereign God? What do we know of it in our own experience?

4. What does ch.18 teach us about the offering, and acceptance, of advice?

5. What may we learn from 19:5,6 (compare Judg. 8:23) about the nature of God's rule? How does this operate in our own individual and church lives?

6. How may God's name be taken in vain today?

7. In what sense is love to God and love to man the complete fulfilment of the Law (Mark 12:28-33)?

21:1-17 The right of slaves

Whilst there are many connections between the laws of Moses and the law-codes of the Fertile Crescent (of which Hammurabi, dated c.1700 BC, is the best-known) the essential difference is the humanity which characterises the former. It is by no means incidental that, in the Book of the Covenant, immediately following the initial revelation and commandments concerning worship (20:21-26), the primary concern is with slaves (1-11). There is no specific appeal to the covenant relationship, but the fact that Israel, once enslaved, had been redeemed by God's saving action, provides the background to this legislation (compare Deut. 5:15; also Matt. 18:23-35). In fact, within Israel, slavery is almost a misnomer, as the maximum legal period of compulsory service was six years (Lev. 25:39,43), although there are many hints in the Old Testament that, due to vested interests, the legislation concerning the sabbath year was not always observed (e.g. 2 Chron. 36:21). Probably a twofold ceremony is indicated in v.6; 'bring him to God' suggests the sanctuary, whereas the 'doorpost' would more naturally refer to the home as the place of future service. The anointing of the right ear of a priest (Exod. 29:20) has a similar connotation of consecration to obedience (see also Ps. 40:6).

The rights of a female slave were particularly safeguarded (7-11). The spirit of this legislation is summed up in the expression 'he shall deal with her as with a daughter' (9), which, with the possibility of a loving attachment which removed the sting of servitude (5), meant that, in Israel, slavery had little of its traditional, evil associations. It is in this setting that the Christian, like Paul, can reckon himself 'a slave of Jesus Christ' (Rom. 1:1, RSV margin) and, for Christ's sake, to be slave to all (2 Cor. 4:5).

Four cases punishable by death are enumerated (12-17). The first (12-14) distinguishes between premeditated murder and manslaughter, and allows time for considered reflection before any judgement is carried out, thus obviating the possibility of uncontrolled blood revenge (compare Deut. 19:1-13). Verses 15 and 17 are connected with parents, and deal with inward attitude as well as actions. Slave-trading (16) was particularly prevalent in the ancient world because it presented an easy way for the powerful to make money quickly at the expense of the poor and weak. Amos condemns two flagrant examples of this abuse (Amos 1:6,9).

QUESTION: Which groups in today's world are especially vulnerable to exploitation? Have we a responsibility to protect them?

21:18-22:17 Restitution

The comprehensive nature of these regulations is remarkable, and allows for an application of basic principles of justice to be applied in cases not specifically covered. It is apparent that a distinction is made between the life of a slave (20,21,32) and a freeman; also, an unborn child is not reckoned as an individual in any sense (22), whilst an unmarried daughter is reckoned as the property of her father (17). Otherwise the main principles have an abiding relevance. They are: (a) Compensation must take into account the degree of impairment of health and the period of convalescence (18,19). (b) Punishment must be related to the crime. Verses 23-25 precluded excessive revenge and were a distinct advance on contemporary practice. In fact, *compensation* was allowed except in the case of murder (Num. 35:31) and false witness, where *intention*, rather than actual deed, was in mind (Deut. 19:15-21). (c) The degree of guilt is increased by any foreknowledge of dangerous tendencies (29,36) or negligence (33,34). (d) In cases of theft it is not enough simply to repay (1-4,7). The theft of an ox (1) was more serious than that of a sheep, not only because it was more valuable, but because it involved a man's livelihood. To kill or sell a stolen animal made the crime more serious. Nathan's judgement on David is an interesting example of the application of the principle involved here (2 Sam. 12:1-15). (e) The death of a burglar in daytime (2,3) is viewed differently because, first, assistance would have been more readily available and, secondly, his identity could have been more easily established, so that he could have been brought to trial. (f) There is an allowable difference of responsibility when an item has been entrusted for care (10-12), borrowed (14), or hired together with its owner (15), a further distinction being made when the person receiving is in no way responsible (13).

To 'come near to God' (8,9) to determine guilt or innocence presumably involved the use of the priestly oracle. The sanctity of an oath made before God is evident (11), and shows how real God was to both parties. It was to be taken seriously, not as a mere formality, as is often the case in legal procedure today.

A REMINDER: Christ, by his teaching, example and sacrifice modified parts of this legislation (e.g. Matt. 5:38,39; Gal. 3:28).

22:18-23:19 Consecrated men.

The evident lack of systematisation in this section of the Book of the Covenant probably witnesses to its early date and sanctity; a later fabrication would doubtless have been more orderly. Many of the laws are of the 'apodictic' type noted earlier, terse and unconditional. Many are amplified elsewhere in later sections of the Pentateuch. The key to the entire section is 22:31a – a consecrated people must have corresponding moral standards.

Complete dedication to God is necessary. This involves absolute separation from idolatry and heathen customs (22:18,20;23:13,19b). God is so uniquely unrivalled that any recognition of, or compromise with, heathenism in any form is unpardonable. Stewardship was to be joyous and spontaneous, *not* grudging (22:29a;23:19; compare 2 Cor. 9:7). The dedication required here is particularly illustrated in the presentation of the first-born (22:29b,30) *in lieu* of the first-born who were spared at the time of Passover (Num. 3:13).

Compassion must be shown to strangers and the underprivileged (22:21-24;23:9). Always they were to bear in mind their own background of bondage. The despairing agony of their own distress (e.g. 2:23) ought to have made them sensitive to the needs of others (but compare Isa. 1:17,23; Jer. 7:5-7).

Within the covenant community there must be brotherliness (22:25-27;23:10,11). This was to extend even to the animals of their enemies (23:4,5). Those properly related to God are also related to each other, like the spokes of a wheel. John stresses the same point in the New Testament (1 John 4: 20,21).

A separated people must have distinct standards. This, inevitably, involved negative aspects (22:19,31). But true religion is much more than a series of prohibitions. Foremost among the positive aspects in this section is the unswerving pursuit of justice without fear or favour (23:1-3, 6-8; compare Deut. 16:20). The man of God must show complete integrity.

Note: The *harvest* connections of Israel's principal feasts are evident (23:14-17). Only the first (Unleavened Bread/Passover, 15) has a historical connection, although later the 'feast of harvest' (16a, or Weeks) was traditionally connected with the giving of the Law at Sinai, and the 'feast of ingathering' (16b, or Tabernacles or Booths) celebrated the wilderness period.

THOUGHT: 'You know the heart of a stranger' (23:9). How does this apply to the Christian?

23:20-33 The principle of Israel's history

The focus of attention now switches to the future. The principle that obedience leads to blessing, whilst disobedience brings disaster is frequently called 'Deuteronomic', since it is most clearly expressed in that book. In fact, it is also found throughout the Old Testament. Experience shows that those who co-operate with God, mindful of his wise commands and living in harmony with others and their environment, *usually* prosper. Later Israel ran into grave difficulties when a stereotyped theology attempted to force a general principle into an inflexible equation which allowed no exception. Job, Jeremiah and the Psalmists called into question or violently attacked this perversion (e.g. Job 21:1-26; Ps. 73; Jer. 12:1-4). Incidentally, the Book of the Covenant, like contemporary secular covenants, ends with a series of blessings and warnings.

The blessings promised are protection (20), guidance (20,23), preparation (20,27), success in war (22,31), prosperity, health, fertility and longevity (26), and national security (31). Only during the reigns of David and Solomon were Israel's frontiers to approximate to the ideal of v.31. This was because the conditions outlined here were not met. Israel failed to give complete obedience (21,22) and uncompromising separation *from* evil (24,32,33) *to* the Lord (25), and the warnings of these verses were largely unheeded. If only Israel had been more obedient!

Two problems of identity emerge: (*a*) *'An angel'* or 'messenger' (20-23). The personal nature of the references seems to exclude an identity with the impersonal ark, or column of smoke/fire. The reference could be to Moses or Joshua, but 'my name is in him' (21) appears to indicate a divine being. Probably there is an oblique reference to the activity of *God himself*, operating directly or through any of the other suggested alternatives. (*b*) *'Hornets'* (28) could be taken literally, although there is no historical evidence for any massive plague. Or it could refer to Egyptian raids or policy which weakened the Canaanites' capacity to resist a major invasion. Many, however, see the hornets interpreted in verse 27 as that divinely inspired panic which paralysed the inhabitants of Canaan (Josh. 2:9,11;5:1).

Note:. Verse 24, 'pillars'. These were upright stone pillars associated with the fertility rites of the Canaanite shrines.

QUESTION: What qualifications would you make to the view that obedience to God always results in blessing?

24 The covenant sealed

The solemn ratification of the covenant indicated here connects firmly with contemporary procedure, and is a further indication of the antiquity of the record. The committing to writing (4), the public reading and unreserved acceptance (7), and the special manipulation of the blood (6,8), all witness to the seriousness of the occasion. God, represented by the elders (9), and the people (8) are symbolically conjoined by sharing in the one blood, and by their participation in a sacramental meal (5,11).

For a short period in Israel's history there was complete unity in promising obedience to the Lord and his requirements (3,7; compare Deut. 5:27-29). This is the 'honeymoon' period referred to by Hosea and Jeremiah (Hos. 2:14,15;9:10a; Jer. 2:2,3), who both look back nostalgically to an initial, brief period of purity in Israel's relationship with God. Unfortunately, it was all too short-lived; indeed, of those who were specially privileged here, Nadab and Abihu (1), were soon to be destroyed because of their unforgivable presumption (Lev. 10:1-3), whilst Aaron and Hur (14) were to fail in the temporary leadership entrusted to them (ch.32). There was, however, no element of failure in Joshua, who is mentioned here for the second time (13; compare 17:8-13).

The two theophanies (10,15-17) are typical of the Old Testament, in that more is concealed than revealed, suggesting God's ultimate inscrutability. Thus there is no conflict with 33:20. In the first (10), reference is made solely to the dais on which God stood, whilst the cloud and fire (15-17), like the 'thick darkness' (see e.g. Ps. 97:2), more than hint at God's 'hiddenness'.

Notes: Verse 1: The gradations here may be paralleled by the arrangements in the Garden of Gethsemane, where Peter, James and John occupy an intermediate position (Matt. 26:36-46) with our Lord, like Moses, being isolated as the mediator of the new covenant (Matt. 26:28). Verse 3, 'words . . . ordinances'. The former probably relates to the unconditional apodictic laws, the latter to detailed examples, the casuistic or case law. Verse 5, 'young men'. Traditional Jewish scholarship usually refers this to the first-born sons of the elders, not to random choice. A certain dexterity and physical agility were required to secure sacrificial animals whilst retaining dignity, hence the selection of a more agile group.

THOUGHT: Verse 11: 'chief men' is literally 'corner pegs'. What does this suggest about the functions of these men?

Questions for further study and discussion on Exodus chapters 21-24

1. 'We are not under law but under grace' (Rom. 6:15). What part does law play in a Christian society?

2. In today's world, is there any point in an oath being taken before evidence is given in a court of law?

3. Are there ways in which the principles of Old Testament legislation should be taken into greater account when forming modern penal laws? What place, for instance, should be given to restitution?

4. Do the interconnections between religion and morality in the book of the covenant have a relevance for Christianity?

5. What is the relationship between the positive and negative aspects of faith?

6. In 23:24, was there justification for such an uncompromising attitude? Is there any situation in which a Christian should be similarly forthright?

7. Compare and contrast Moses' part in the old covenant and Christ's in the new.

25 The pattern of the tabernacle

Three basic principles of stewardship emerge (1-9). (*a*) The giver must have a willing heart (2; 2 Cor. 9:7). (*b*) No limit is set on what may be offered to God. Verses 3-7 range from precious commodities to items of everyday use. God does not despise the gifts of the poor (compare Luke 21:1-4). (*c*) Stewardship should be for God-directed projects (8,9).

In the directions for the tabernacle the starting point is not the dwelling itself, but the highly-significant *furniture* of the holy of holies and the holy place. In the central shrine there was the *ark*, the *mercy seat* and the *cherubim* (10-22). The ark was the supreme covenant symbol. Unlike contemporary arks in neighbouring countries, it contained no representation of the deity, only the tablets of the law (16), a jar of manna (16:33), and Aaron's rod (Num. 17:10) – all symbolic of the Lord's provision. The cherubim, joined by the slab of solid gold which formed the mercy seat (17), formed a throne for the invisible Yahweh, Israel's God (22), the covering wings of the cherubim (20) representing the divine protection (compare Ruth 2:12). The mercy seat (Heb. *kapporeth*) derived from the verb 'to make atonement', and was symbolically sprinkled with blood on the great annual Day of Atonement (Lev. 16:14). The ark, being placed *under* the mercy seat (21), formed God's footstool (Pss. 99:1,5;132:7,8) and highlighted the fact that the Law was under God's protection. In contrast to Jeroboam's golden calves (1 Kings 12:28,29), which were probably pedestals on which the invisible God was thought to stand, the cherubim were supra-terrestial beings. The calves of Jeroboam reproduced the main Canaanite fertility symbol.

In the holy place there was the *table of incense* and the *golden lampstand* (23-40). Leviticus 24:5-8 gives fuller detail concerning 'the bread of the Presence' (30), which probably represented God's daily provision for all his people – hence the *twelve* baked cakes. The golden lampstand, throughout Scripture, speaks of the witness of the covenant community (see e.g. Zech 4:1-7; Rev. 2:1). The attention to detail is remarkable. The lamps required regular servicing or the light would grow dim. Mention is made of the instruments for this mundane task (38) which were to be made of *pure gold*.

MEDITATION: The tabernacle was (*a*) God's dwelling (8); (*b*) the 'tent of meeting' (22a); and (*c*) the place of communication (22b). Compare John 14:23.

The Tabernacle

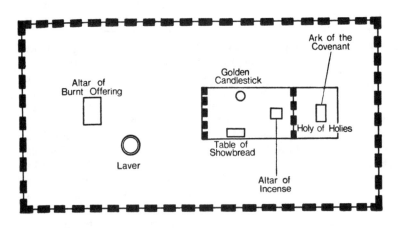

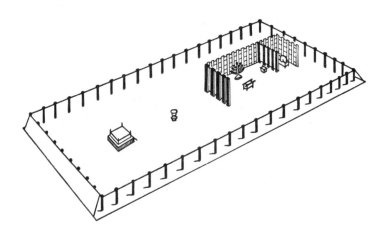

26 Constructional details

In the remaining section of the book there is considerable duplication, with the specification for the tabernacle given in chs. 25-27;30, its construction in chs. 36-38, and its actual erection in ch. 40. This, however, serves to underline its importance. The tabernacle itself was not imperishable; archaeological evidence suggests that it was destroyed by the Philistines c.1050 BC, soon after the double defeat recorded in 1 Sam. 4. The basic details, however, were incorporated into Solomon's and Zerubbabel's temples, and do have a continuing significance in men's approach to God (e.g. Heb. 9).

The overall dimensions of the sanctuary itself were roughly 44 ft × 15 ft × 15 ft (14 m × 5 m × 5 m), allowing for a cubit of 17.49 inches. The veil (33) curtained off the 15 ft × 15 ft (5 m × 5 m) holy of holies, and the cherubim embroidered thereon (31) served as the guardians of the inner shrine. The only items of furniture in the holy of holies were the ark, mercy seat and cherubim (34). A further curtain screened the entrance to the holy place (36), where only the priests were allowed. All the detail concerning the overlapping curtains, the tightly secured joints (e.g. 10,11), and the top, waterproof covering (14), emphasises how dark and isolated the interior must have been. The God who dwelt in thick darkness (e.g. Ps. 97:2) must be preserved from prying eyes. A further overall impression must have been one of great beauty.

The tabernacle, in fact, was a model of precision construction. Earlier generations of critical scholars frequently viewed it as a post-exilic figment of the imagination, based on Solomon's Temple, holding that anything as elaborate as this would be inconceivable at an earlier date. But archaeological evidence for portable, pre-fabricated shrines and throne-rooms, employing similar constructional techniques to the tabernacle, in Egypt (where Israel had been for generations), for hundreds of years before the period of Moses, has made such scepticism unreasonable. The main advantages of this type of construction were portability, durability and ease of erection and dismantling. God was not confined to Sinai; he was a God 'on the move', guiding and accompanying his people (compare 2 Sam. 7:5-7).

QUESTION: What significance do the elements of separation, beauty and portability have for us today?

27 The outer court

As we move from the tabernacle itself to its outer court we notice that the materials used change from gold to bronze or silver, and from costly fabrics (26:31) to more everyday materials (9). There is an obvious significance in this. The altar (1-8), usually called the 'altar of burnt offering' (30:28) to distinguish it from the altar of incense (30:1-10), stood between the tabernacle and the eastern 'gate', which was simply a 29 ft (9 m) screened opening, a reminder that there could be no access to God except via the altar. The overall dimensions of the outer court, which marked off the area sacred to the Lord, were 146 ft × 73 ft (45 m × 22 m), the curtaining, being a little over 7 ft (2 m) high, preventing it from being overlooked.

The altar itself was approximately 7 ft × 7 ft × 4 ft 3 ins (2 m × 2 m × 1.25 m), a hollow, wooden framework overlaid with bronze, and so easily transportable. The permanent altar in Solomon's Temple, in contrast, covered an area sixteen times larger (2 Chron. 4:1). The purpose of the grating (4,5) is not clear: it could have extended around the lower, outer sides of the altar, so providing draught for the sacrificial fire; or it could have been *inside* the altar at the half-way point, like a modern barbecue-stove. The horns (2) may originally have symbolised the sacrificial animals themselves, but their continuing function was to facilitate the securing of the beasts. The one who sought sanctuary by clinging to the horns of the altar (e.g. 1 Kings 1:50) was, symbolically, surrendering himself as a sacrifice to the Lord and so claiming his protection. Some scholars believe that, in line with 20:24, the altar was partly filled with earth, which would soak up the blood.

The lamp (20,21) was probably the seven-branched candlestick (25:31-37), as there is no legislation for any other illumination in the holy place. One of the priestly functions was to tend this (21; compare 1 Sam. 3:3), using the golden snuffers and placing the carbon deposits from the trimmed lamps in the trays provided (25:38) – thus avoiding any soiling of the sanctuary or the priestly garments. The best-quality oil would ensure the brightest possible light (20).

QUESTION: Does the care given to the lamp suggest anything concerning the witness of God's people?

28 The priestly garments

The main concern is with the garments of Aaron (1-39), those of the other priests being of a more utilitarian nature (40-43). This is understandable in a community bound together in a religious relationship with God which focused on a central sanctuary – their chief functionary should be attired in a way which stressed his 'apartness' (2), using the choicest materials (5). The main garment was the ephod (6-14), and the breast piece of judgement which was securely attached to it (15-30). Scholars are unsure, from the description here, whether the ephod was a type of kilt or waistcoat. The uncertainty is compounded elsewhere because the ephod seems to indicate a free-standing image (e.g. Judg. 8:24-27;17:5). The one certainty is that the ephod was always concerned with ascertaining God's will (e.g. 1 Sam. 23:9-12). The Urim and Thummim (30), used in this connection, were probably flat, inscribed stones which could be withdrawn either singly or together from the pouch-like breast piece, the possible combinations representing simple alternatives to the question posed, such as 'yes', 'no' or 'uncertain'. Proverbs 16:33 indicates God's overruling of a method which seems haphazard, but which was still used in apostolic times (Acts 1:23-26; although Urim and Thummim had long since disappeared, e.g. Ezra 2:63). The descent of the Holy Spirit (Acts 2) made possible a direct, divine revelation. Both the ephod and the breast piece incorporated memories of the twelve tribes (9-12,17-21), symbolically carried into the Lord's presence, indicating the mediatorial, representative function of the high priest.

Of Aaron's four sons (1), two, Nadab and Abihu, who had already been especially privileged (24:1), were to perish for their presumption (Lev. 10:1-3). Aaron's line, therefore, continued through Eleazar and Ithamar (Num. 3:1-4). There may have been a power struggle between the two families, with the line of Eleazar, from which the Zadokites descended (1 Chron. 6:4-8,49-53), ultimately triumphing, although Eli and Abiathar, David's friends of Ithamar's line (1 Sam. 22:20; 1 Chron. 24:3), appear to be dominant for a considerable period.

QUESTION: Does v.3 suggest anything about the exaggerated distinction often made between intellectual and manual skills?

29 Consecration of priests and altar

There were three operations in the ordination of Aaron and his sons; first they were washed (4), then ceremonially robed (5-9), and finally consecrated by sacrifice (10-34). The repetition over a seven-day period (35-37) emphasises the solemnity and significance of the occasion. It was no light thing to serve and represent the living God.

The first sacrifice (10-14) was a *sin-offering*, a reminder that the priesthood, though privileged, was subject to sin like everyone else. The cleansing of the priesthood, annually, on the Day of Atonement (Lev.16:6), ensured that the fallibility of God's representatives was not forgotten. In this and the second sacrifice the placing of the hands on the heads of the animals (10,15) signified an identification with the animal substitute. The *whole burnt offering* (15-18) indicated the total consecration of the priesthood to its task. The third sacrifice (19-28) was within the class of *peace-offerings*, suitably modified for the occasion. The essence of this type was that it was partly eaten by the worshipper and so signified communion with God and therefore acceptance by him. Part of this sacrifice was a 'wave offering' (24), a ritual manipulation which emphasised that it belonged to God. Normally it would then be eaten by the priests as God's representatives, but here it was devoted to God, to stress the fact that their first sacrificial offering to him had been accepted (25). A corresponding ceremony for the cleansing and consecration of the altar as the place of approach to God was also incorporated into the seven-day ceremony (37).

The *continual burnt-offering* (38-42) ought to have provided a twice-daily reminder of Israel's need and God's mercy; unfortunately, like many religious practices, it degenerated into a mere formality. The covenant, the essence of which is stated in vs.45,46, became simply a matter of outward observance. Jeremiah recognised this and pointed the way forward to a *new* covenant (Jer. 31:31-34).

QUESTION: Is there significance for us in the application of the cleansing, consecrating blood to the ear (obedience?), hand (actions?), food, and dress of the priests (20,21)?

30 Supplementary specifications

The altar of incense (1-10) is here mentioned for the first time, possibly to highlight the importance of the altar for sacrifice (often referred to simply as '*the* altar', e.g. 18,20) in the main legislation (27:1-8). The former is often called the 'golden altar' (e.g. 40:5) to distinguish it from the sacrificial bronze altar. Verse 6 could be read as implying that the altar of incense was *within* the holy of holies (compare Heb. 9:4), but 40:1-5,20-27 make it clear that it was in the holy place, before the veil, and between the table of showbread and the lampstand.

In the ancient world, and amongst primitive people today, and as late as the eighteenth century in Britain, it was considered dangerous to take a census (compare 2 Sam. 24). A compulsory ransom payment, binding on all without distinction (11-16), was levied to secure protection from God's anger. In Nehemiah's time (Neh. 10:32) the tax was reduced to one-third of a shekel. Assuming that this referred to the lighter Babylonian (as opposed to the Phoenician) shekel, this was about *half* the amount required here and in New Testament times (Matt. 17:24). Probably this reduction was due to the considerable poverty in the early post-exilic period.

It is surprising that no specifications are given for the bronze laver (17-21; compare 1 Kings 7:23-26,38,39). It was made of the mirrors of the 'ministering women' (38:8), and served as a reminder of that cleanliness, inward and external, necessary before undertaking any service for the Lord.

Anointing was regularly associated with consecration to a task or function, and with healing. It also had a 'secular' use as a cosmetic. The anointing oil (22-33) was made of the finest imported ingredients: myrrh from Arabia; cinnamon and cassia (derived from cinnamon bark) from China; and aromatic cane from India. Everything connected with the tabernacle was anointed except the mercy seat and cherubim, which represented God's throne. As with the incense (37,38), there was to be no secular use of this recipe (31-33); it was reserved exclusively for the Lord. Incense originally meant something which went up from the sacrifice, which the deity could smell and, in a sense, assimilate (e.g. Gen. 8:21). It also served to veil God from human eyes (Lev. 16:13). At an early date it signified the prayers of the faithful (Psa. 141:2; compare Rev. 5:8;8:3,4).

QUESTION: Why was everyone on the same footing (14,15)?

31 Work and rest

The plans of God require human implementation, and this goes beyond the leadership of men like Moses and Aaron. A considerable range of skills was necessary if the details for the tabernacle and priesthood were to be worked out, and God the architect is seen as the source of such craftsmanship (1-11). Bezalel (2) and his assistant, Oholiab, are specifically named, but there was a vast, nameless company of skilled workers in support (6). We have here an illustration of the way in which men can co-operate with God, with their various, God-given abilities complementing each other, and of the final result of such God-initiated, God-directed projects. A similar unity in diversity is seen in the functioning of the New Testament church (e.g. Rom. 12:3-8; 1 Cor. 12:4-26), of which Christ is the head (Eph. 1:22-23). Bezalel was allowed to express his own individual creativity (4) within the limits of the overall mandate (11).

The final section of God's direct revelation to Moses underlines and amplifies the previous instruction concerning the Sabbath (20:8-11;23:12). There is a significance in this, for Sabbath observance involved a *continual* honouring of God, unlike circumcision, the other great covenant sign, which was a once-in-a-lifetime act performed at the instigation of one's parents, although with spiritual implications which were often overlooked (see Jer. 4:4;9:25,26). It required tenacity of purpose and faith to keep the Sabbath consistently, avoiding the kind of duplicity which Amos, Jeremiah and Nehemiah condemned (Amos 8:4-6; Jer. 17:19-23; Neh. 13:15-18). Hence Sabbath-observance became a barometer of the spirituality of the nation or individual (see Ezek. 20:12-24). Isaiah 58:13,14 expresses the essence of a positive, God-honouring attitude toward the Sabbath. It should also be remembered that it was not simply a case of one day in seven being given to God. The Sabbath was an acknowledgment that the whole week belonged to him; it consecrated the whole. Man's responsibility is to honour him in the use of all seven days.

Note: Verse 18. In a section full of God-given legislation, this verse emphasises the unique sanctity attaching to the ten commandments.

THOUGHT: 'The Lord . . . was refreshed' (17). To what extent ought this to result from our use of Sunday?

Questions for further study and discussion on Exodus chapters 25-31

1. Is there any apparent reason why some items in the tabernacle were made of 'pure gold' and others of gold which presumably included some alloy?

2. Is it justifiable to look for a spiritual significance in every detail of the tabernacle? What is the place of symbolism in modern church architecture?

3. Consider the connection between Ps. 132:9 (and Exod. 28:2,36) and 1 Pet. 2:9;3:3,4;5:5.

4. What are the principal differences between the Old Covenant (e.g. 29:45) and the New (Jer. 31:31-34; Heb. 8:7-13)?

5. With the aid of a concordance if necessary, trace the place and purpose of anointing in the Old Testament. What are modern equivalents?

6. Does 30:17-21 have any parallel in Christian service?

7. Are there dangers in both over-stressing or over-emphasising the connections between the Jewish Sabbath and the Christian Sunday? What are the lasting principles which should control our conduct?

32 The shattered covenant

Israel's early failure might seem inexplicable were it not for our personal awareness of the frailty of human nature. Israel had been spectacularly delivered; she had encountered God at Sinai and had solemnly promised obedience (19:8;24:7). How soon it evaporated (compare Hos. 6:4)! Their desire for a visual focus for worship is not unique, but the Lord's part in their deliverance, even the experience itself as a deliverance, seems to have been forgotten (1). 'Calf' (4) is rather misleading; 'young bull' would be more accurate, referring to the chief symbol of Baal and the main image of procreative power. *'Play'* (6) likewise appears innocuous, but in fact it refers to sex-play, and in conjunction with vs.17-19,25, describes a drunken, licentious orgy typical of the Canaanite Baal worship.

Aaron's leadership also appears weak to the point of non-existence. He timidly went along with the people's demands (2) and personally hand-sculptured the image, in the light of which his later suggestion of a miraculous production (24) appears pathetic. Probably he was sincere in his desire to retain the worship of the Lord (5), although it is doubtful whether the people shared this, but the whole episode reveals his spineless compromise.

Moses' true greatness, as the shepherd of Israel and an intercessor passionately loyal to God, shines out. A great honour was offered him, which would have made him a second Abraham or Jacob (10b; compare Gen. 12:2;35:11). His selfless concern, however, was for: (a) the completion of God's work (11); (b) God's honour in the contemporary world (12); and (c) the fulfilment of God's promises (13). 'Repentance' (14), as applied to God, does not involve a change of mind from a wrongful position, as with us. It is rather a change of attitude made possible by a change in circumstances. This involves no inconsistency of character, and illustrates the place and power of Moses' intercession. Clearly Moses expected a serious judgement beyond the resolute action of the Levites in the immediate crisis (25-29), for in the legislation already given the seriousness of disobedience had been repeatedly stressed. His intercessory concern (30-32) parallels that of Abraham (Gen. 18:22-33). But no man, be he Moses, David (2 Sam. 18:33), or Paul (Rom. 9:3), can be a substitute for the sins of others. That can only be done by Christ (e.g. Rom. 5:6-9).

MEDITATION: '. . . Apart from me you can do nothing' (John 15:5).

33 Face to face fellowship

Verses 1-6 amount to a virtual ejection from God's presence at Sinai. This marked his displeasure, but was, in a sense, for Israel's protection (3,5; compare Heb. 12:29). 'Stiff-necked', a farming metaphor, is particularly appropriate here, as it indicates the unresponsiveness of an animal to the controlling, guiding rope of its master. The non-wearing of ornaments (4,6), a mark of mourning, would be a reminder of this judgement. Nevertheless, God's angel (2; compare 32:34) would precede Israel and guarantee their success and inheritance in the promised land (3).

Verses 7-11. The 'tent' was the precursor of the tabernacle, and its place outside the camp, temporarily, was evidently a further punishment (compare Num. 2, where the tabernacle is again central). Here Moses alone enjoyed a personal fellowship with God unequalled elsewhere in the Old Testament (9,11), acting vicariously for the people (8,10). How much they had forfeited by their sin! Almost incidentally we observe how Joshua was being groomed for future leadership (11b).

Verses 12-16. All who experience the wonder and joy of fellowship with God can appreciate Moses' deep yearning for yet more (compare Ps. 63:1-4). His plea is on the basis of an existing personal relationship (12b), and his request is for guidance so that he, in turn, might adequately shepherd God's people (13). Twice God had promised the presence of his angel, without disclosing his identity (12). This has given rise to many scholarly conjectures, ranging from the ark to Moses' father-in-law (Num. 10:29-32). God appears to go further in reassuring Moses that his presence (lit. 'face') would go with him. It could indicate something less than the full presence of God, but in context this is unlikely, since Moses stresses that the divine presence, supremely, distinguishes Israel from all other nations (16). If this interpretation be correct it means that the Lord had negated the limited assurance of vs.1-6. Such graciousness, on God's part, would explain Moses' boldness in the next section.

Verses 17-23. God's *'glory'* and *'goodness'* (18,19) are probably to be equated. Moses longs for the fullest possible token of God's favour, but even he could not have endured God's total majesty and holiness. ·However, he actually heard Yahweh himself pronounce his name (19), and he saw, fleetingly, the fringes of the retreating glory. Significantly, no description of the indescribable is preserved.

QUESTION: 'Blessed are the pure in heart, for they shall see God' (Matt. 5:8). How does this relate to Moses and ourselves?

34 The covenant renewed

Through the mediation of Moses, but principally because of God's faithfulness and graciousness, the way was now open for the covenant relationship to be restored. But this was not achieved lightly; the length of time was the same (28; compare 24:18), and the precautions for Moses' isolation were similar (2-5; compare 24:1,2,12-18). The opening of God's address (6,7) forms the greatest theological statement on his nature in the Old Testament. These verses, in whole or part, are often quoted elsewhere. Each word or phrase invites a pause for meditation, but the repeated 'steadfast love' (Heb. *chesed*) is the great covenantal word, speaking of God's faithfulness and love. It occurs some 270 times in the Old Testament.

Moses' plea, and his ready admission of Israel's failure and weakness (9), found God prompt to respond (10-26). There was no need to repeat all that had been previously delivered; the ten commandments, for instance, were rewritten but not restated (28). The covenant *was* renewed, together with the assurance of God's continuing, powerful activity (10,11). However, in the light of Israel's conspicuous failure while still at the mountain of revelation, God gave clear warning of what they were to avoid when in the promised land (11-26). There was to be no compromise of any kind with heathen religion; no covenants or intermarriage with their heathen neighbours. Israel failed miserably in each of these areas (e.g. Judg. 2:11-3:6;10:6; Ezra 9:1,2), and so failed to realise God's promised blessings. The exclusive devotion to their Redeemer-God demanded here was conspicuously absent.

This section is often called the 'Ritual Decalogue' in contradistinction to the 'Ethical Decalogue' (20:1-17), because of its preoccupation with cultic affairs. It is thought, by some, to be 'primitive' and earlier than Exod. 20, which, of course, contradicts the biblical sequence of events. However, it is by no means certain that there *are* ten commandments in this section; most scholars divide the material into twelve or thirteen. It is preferable to regard this as a restressing of certain elements in the light of recent events and the peculiar temptations which Israel would confront in Canaan.

Moses, as a result of his fellowship with God, became the man with the shining face (29,35). However, this was to fade, in contrast to the Christian's permanent glory (2 Cor. 3:7-18). Unlike Moses, we need no veil.

MEDITATION: Psalm 34:5.

35:1-36:38 The will to work

The material in these and subsequent chapters repeats the earlier detail and calls for little additional comment. The duplication, however, is of value in indicating Moses' faithful adherence to his commission. The Lord had commanded, 'According to all that I have commanded you they shall do' (31:11) – here we see the diligent outworking of this.

We also gain an impression of a community united in a common task which they pursued energetically and sacrificially. All classes were involved: some gave the raw materials to be used for the tabernacle and its accessories; others gave of their skills; others, like the master-architects, Bezalel and Oholiab (35:30-35), instructed others. The outcome was an embarrassing over-abundance (36:2-7) – a problem God's people have rarely had to face. Such is the result when stewardship comes from the heart prompted by God's Spirit (e.g. 35:5,21); it becomes something joyous, not a matter of cold, precise calculation. An Old Testament parallel is the diverse groups who shared in the building of the wall of Jerusalem, and the amazing success of that enterprise (Neh. 3:1,8,12,17,32;6:15). In the New Testament the joyous, sacrificial giving of the Macedonian Christians, in spite of their extreme poverty, invites comparison (2 Cor. 8:1-5).

The repetition of the detail for the observance of the Sabbath may seem an intrusion in this section (35:1-3). Its inclusion doubtless results from the danger of over-enthusiasm by the Israelites in the tabernacle-project. It would have been easy to rationalise the situation – after all, it *was* the Lord's work they were about, why not use the Lord's day for it? But the Sabbath was sacrosanct. Does this have any bearing on the Christian's use of Sunday?

THOUGHT: '. . . First they gave themselves to the Lord' (2 Cor. 8:5). Is this the cardinal principle of stewardship?

37:1-38:31 Craftsmen at work

There is a logical order of construction here, which contrasts with the earlier legislation. In both the commencing point is the tabernacle, but in this section the *structure* of the tabernacle was made first (36:8-38), before its furniture (37:1-38:8). In the detail of the construction of the latter, however, the ark, mercy seat and cherubim are again given priority. The significance of these, as the throne of the invisible God, the only items to be placed in the holy of holies, has already been noted. The altar of incense is grouped with the other articles in the holy place (37:25-28), in contrast to its detachment in the earlier section (30:1-5), and the oil and incense to be used in connection with the tabernacle is also included (37:29; compare 30:22-38).

The inclusion of certain items suggests that the actual account was written or rewritten at a later date. For instance, the mention of Levites (38:21) anticipates their appointment in Num. 3. A certain grouping is also evident in 37:1, since the ark itself, as a wooden receptacle for the law-tablets, had already been made (Deut. 10:1-3, where 'I made an ark' is probably to be understood in a causative sense, 'I caused to be made'). There is no conflict between 38:2 and Num. 16:39,40. Obviously a wooden-framed altar required a metal overlay, so the Numbers reference must be read as either an extra overlay or a canopy of some kind.

The final tally of metals used in the construction of the tabernacle and its accessories was impressive (38:24-31), amounting approximately to a ton of gold, three tons of copper and four tons of silver. The surprisingly large amount of silver is explained by the compulsory half-shekel offering detailed in 30:11-16.

Note: 38:8, 'the ministering women'. The suggestion, occasionally made, that these were cult-prostitutes after the Canaanite pattern is unwarranted (*a*) in view of the high ethical standards laid down by God, and (*b*) in the light of the horrified condemnation of such a practice in 1 Sam. 2:22-25. It is surely reasonable to suppose that there were ministries associated with the tabernacle which women were better equipped to perform.

QUESTION: Can you think of (and account for) other instances of 'repetition' (even fourfold, e.g. the feeding of the 5000) in Scripture?

39:1-40:38 God's glory with his people

The further repetitions which occur serve to underline once more the sanctity and solemnity of this phase in Israel's history. As firmly emphasised is the total obedience of Moses, summed up in 40:16. Seven times in the section dealing with the making of the priestly vestments (39:1-31) Moses' obedience is mentioned (1,5,7,21,26,29,31), and a further seven times in the erection of the tabernacle and the placing of its accessories (40:19,21,23,25,27,29,32). This recurrence of the 'perfect number' is probably not accidental. The total value of the whole is incalculable, and yet every item had been made possible by the donations of mainly poor people recently delivered from slavery. Fittingly, the erection of the tabernacle marked the first anniversary of the deliverance from Egypt (40:1,2,17).

God had promised, '. . . let them make me a sanctuary, that I may dwell in their midst' (25:8). The people had fulfilled their part; now God honoured his commitment (40:34-38). In a way which was paralleled in the dedication of Solomon's Temple (1 Kings 8:10,11) 'the glory of the Lord filled the tabernacle' (34). There is invariably a tension in revelation between God's transcendence and his immanence. How can he dwell with men and yet be 'wholly other'? Both aspects of God's being were safeguarded here; he was in the midst of his people, but even Moses was excluded from the tabernacle by reason of God's awesome majesty. Thereafter the cloud and fire would provide a continuing assurance of God's presence and guidance (36-38). We might have expected a triumphant progress to the promised land. Sadly, Israel failed miserably, even with these external signs, and a complete generation perished in the wilderness (Num. 14:26-33). Sometimes we may long for tangible indications of God's presence and direction, but, in fact, we have the far richer promises of Christ's abiding presence (Matt. 28:20) and the Holy Spirit's power (Acts 1:8). G. A. Chadwick comments, 'If the presence is less material, it is because we ought to be more spiritual'.

Note: 39:22,23. The construction of the 'robe of the ephod' was doubtless similar to the robe worn by Christ at his crucifixion (John 19:23), which may hint at his high-priesthood.

QUESTION: In what sense are our bodies the tabernacle or temple of God (see 1 Cor. 3:16,17;6:19,20)?

Questions for further study and discussion on Exodus chapters 32-40

1. How typical is ch.32 of the subsequent history of Israel? What similar dangers do we face? How do we respond?

2. What is the New Testament equivalent to the promises of God's presence in ch.33?

3. In what ways ought a close relationship with God show itself?

4. List any features of (*a*) stewardship, and (*b*) service, which you have found helpful in these chapters.

5. What can we learn for our own church life from the way in which the Israelites set about building the tabernacle?

6. How far is the presence of God's glory in the tabernacle connected with the obedience and enthusiasm of the people in the building? How could we experience more of God's glory in our own lives?

7. What are the principal lessons that God has taught you through the book of Exodus?